40757

BERGEN CO

MAKERS OF MODERN HISTORY

MAKERS OF MODERN HISTORY

THREE TYPES

LOUIS NAPOLEON—CAVOUR—BISMARCK

BY THE HON. EDWARD CADOGAN

KENNIKAT PRESS
Port Washington, N. Y./London

MAKERS OF MODERN HISTORY

First published in 1905
Reissued in 1970 by Kennikat Press
Library of Congress Catalog Card No: 75-112797
ISBN 0-8046-1064-9

Manufactured by Taylor Publishing Company   Dallas, Texas

PREFACE

THE writer of the short Essays contained in this volume feels the necessity, by way of introduction, to explain the objects of the work and to justify the selection of the historical subjects dealt with. "It is the appointed lot," writes Mahan in his admirable biography of Nelson, "of some of history's chosen few to come upon the scene at the moment when a great tendency is nearing its crisis and its culmination. Specially gifted with qualities needed to realise the fulness of its possibilities, they so identify themselves with it by their deeds, that they henceforth personify to the world the movement which brought them forth, and of which their own achievements are at once the climax and the most dazzling illustration." These words apply in every essential to the three men who have been selected as the subjects for the following Essays. The chief interest that attaches to European history during the nineteenth century lies in the great struggle between Conservative principles and the revolutionary forces of constitutional or national liberty, and it is with this great struggle that the illustrious names of Bismarck, Louis Napoleon, and Cavour will ever be associated. These few preliminary remarks, it is hoped, will serve to justify the writer's selection. The biographies of these three men, if drawn out to their full length, and filled in with all detail would, in themselves, constitute an exhaustive history of the period. The following Essays, of course, lay claim to no such distinction. They are merely short studies confessedly introductory, written with the intention of "stimulating rather than satisfying curiosity."

A large amount of matter of extreme importance has been purposely omitted, both in order to preserve the character of the Essays which are only intended to be light sketches, and also to make them more acceptable to those who do not seek for an exhaustive treatise on the workings of foreign Parliaments, but at the same time the writer earnestly hopes that he will be the means of inciting some of his readers to a closer study of the history of the nineteenth century, a knowledge of which is not only deeply interesting but essential to those who would understand the great international problems of the present day.

EDWARD CADOGAN.

CULFORD HALL, *July* 1904.

CONTENTS

	PAGE
LOUIS NAPOLEON	1
CAVOUR	74
BISMARCK	143

MAKERS OF MODERN HISTORY

PART I

LOUIS NAPOLEON

THE questions of morality arising out of all great national movements are many and complicated. The tendency to maintain that certain moral laws are for universal application—without taking into consideration that in certain individual cases the application of these laws would be both impracticable and harmful—has served often to confuse the student of political ethics. During the French Revolution of 1789 Horace Walpole expressed it as his opinion that no great country was ever saved by good men, because good men will not go to the lengths that may be necessary. This maxim embodies the vexed question which for centuries has formed a staple subject of controversy for both the historian and the philosopher, a problem which in our own time seems no nearer a plausible solution. On the one side it has been maintained that any means must be employed to compass the end, provided that the ultimate issue shall prove beneficial to mankind; and on the other side, the narrower political moralist clings with no less tenacity to the doctrine that it were better for the sun and moon to fall from heaven than that one soul should commit one venial sin. These are the two opposite poles of opinion. Shrewd statesmen have often tried to steer a *via media* between the two, but the normal tendency is to draw towards that which seems to hold out the fullest measure of human practicability, and consequently success becomes to the majority the only motive of allegiance in this world. In the striving after this end strict moral principle must be too frequently set aside, and the triumph of a success often smothers in oblivion the ends used in its attainment.

Some four centuries ago Machiavelli outraged the moral sense of Europe by publishing a treatise on statecraft which seemed to offer a logical demonstration that dishonesty is the best policy. In this treatise he deliberately drew the distinction between dishonesty well employed and dishonesty ill employed, and yet the distinction, startling as it seemed to his contemporaries, was not an original one. Rulers and statesmen of all ages have recognised the distinction and have lived up to their recognition of it, subduing the conflicting pangs of an outraged conscience with the quieting reflection that certain ends justify any means. In spite, however, of political sceptics, modern thought, it must be confessed, will not permit the eradication of the idea of right and wrong in politics; but nevertheless it must be borne in mind that neither in our judgments of history nor in our judgments of contemporaries is it possible to apply the full stringency of private morals to the cases of men acting in posts of great responsibility and danger amid the storms of revolution, panic, or civil war; and therefore the question becomes so involved that it is essentially necessary to study all the attendant circumstances of each individual case before it is possible to estimate the extent to which we can palliate the actions of those who, with a total disregard for all moral codes, attain to the object of their ambitions.

There are few better examples of the Machiavellian doctrine than the *coup d'état* of Louis Napoleon. In fact, in its entirety and success it serves even as a better illustration than the tactics of Cesare Borgia, which the author of *The Prince* regards as the beau ideal to be emulated by all those who would found and consolidate a kingdom.

The result has been that few great European movements have caused so much contentious disputation as the overthrowing of the French Constitution and the means by which it was effected on that fateful December evening in the year 1851. If the actions of the Prince President on that occasion are to be ranged before posterity to receive condemnation or acquittal, there is no doubt that the majority must declare against his inconsistency of principle, his sanguinary measures, and his breach of faith; but it would be as idle to pass judgment upon his entire policy because certain of his actions did not tally with convention, as it would be to condemn some salutary medicine because one of the ingredients in the prescription happened to be rank poison. The very expression "*coup d'état*" in this case is misleading: it would seem to imply some sudden and isolated action. No *coup d'état* can be successful unless the former *régime* has proved unpalatable to the people, so that a *coup d'état*, unless it is to be a mere flash in the pan, is, with the majority of cases, the consummation of a long desired change.

It must be admitted, therefore, that while examining this much disputed question of morality in its relation to politics as applied to Louis Napoleon's actions in the year 1851, it would be presumption to condemn him without a thorough knowledge of the attendant circumstances of the case, and of the contemporary history of France. Without exaggeration it may be affirmed that the career of Louis Napoleon is one of the most remarkable in history. It is all the more remarkable because he was a man of distinctly mediocre character, of not unusual ability, and possessed of few of those qualities which constitute a man great in the ordinarily accepted interpretation of the word.

True it is that he was endowed with one eminent advantage from the outset of his career, and he made the most of it. The glamour of his name doubtless contributed in a large measure to his ultimate success, and aided him while striving with the sea of troubles which threatened many times to overwhelm him; yet had it not been for that dogged determination which always constituted the most distinctive feature in his character, he never could have attained the zenith of his ambitions. Moreover, without being endowed with any remarkable intellectual qualities, without exhibiting any particularly able characteristics, he was, at the outset of his career, shrewd enough to seize upon the opportunities that fortune placed in his path; and it should be remembered that fortune rarely offers to mankind anything else than the occasion for carrying designs into effect.

Louis Napoleon early in life discerned this, and acted accordingly; but above all things he believed that a great destiny awaited him, and it might almost be said of him that he was possessed of that faith which we are told in the Scriptures can move the very mountains themselves.

This overweening confidence in Fate, grounded as it seemed to be upon unerring instincts, never forsook him in his darkest hours, and without it he would never have realised what appeared to his friends such preposterous dreams. This belief in himself was the product of an intensely superstitious temperament. It is said that he was wont to try by every conceivable means to lift the veil of the future, and there was not a single fortune-teller of any repute whom he did not consult, and whose predictions did not influence his actions; but although this exaggerated superstition fostered his indifference to danger, it produced at the same time that fatal indecision which becomes apparent in the policy of his later years.

Louis Napoleon loved power for power's sake, and this undoubtedly was the worst trait in his character. The circumstances of his career have served to heap upon his head a mass of unjustifiable slander of which we can readily acquit him, but his true nature must ever remain somewhat of an enigma to the historian. Beneath a certain depth in his character it is impossible to probe. He seems to us a fatuous man of dreams, but although he is not the only man in history who has dreamt his way to power, there are few who, like him, have built such castles in the air and subsequently placed them on foundations, unstable and incomplete though they may have proved to be. No one, however enthusiastic, with any justification can presume to compare him with his great predecessor; but contemporary critics were too apt to despise his character and to pour contempt upon him as a moody exile, as a mere charlatan and a freak of fortune. They were too ready to scoff at him as "*ce faux Napoleon!*" the sport of European Powers. A close study of his career will reveal much that will demolish such a verdict, and although it may serve as a warning to the adventurous in statecraft, it cannot fail to leave a conviction that, with all his glaring faults, he has suffered at the hands of hostile critics more than the circumstances of his life seem to justify.

Louis Napoleon was born in Paris on the 20th April 1808. His cradle was at the Tuileries

Palace, in the closest vicinity to the throne. He was the third son of Louis Buonaparte, one of the king-brothers of the great Emperor, and of Hortense Beauharnais, daughter of the Empress Joséphine by her first husband. The Emperor, with his newly-married Empress Marie Louise, held him at the font, so that his earliest days were spent under Napoleonic auspices, and even after the birth of the " Roi de Rome " he was treated with all the honours due to an heir-presumptive. It is to be concluded, then, that before his exile the great Napoleon saw much of the infant nephew who was destined one day to wield his sceptre and to wear his crown. There is a story told that the young Louis Napoleon clung to his uncle's knees when he was departing from Malmaison for the last time, struggling against separation, as if instinct had told him that with the Emperor his own fortunes and those of the House were overshadowed. After this parting he spent his youth for the most part with his mother at the Castle of Arenenberg on the borders of Lake Constance.

Always of an adventurous disposition he soon found a field for his tastes in the Romagna, where in the year 1831 a revolt had broken out against papal rule. In the same year his eldest brother died, and soon after the " Roi de Rome " succumbed to a fatal malady. These two events placed him at the head of the Napoleonic dynasty, and although to the world this seemed a vacuous position under the existing circumstances, from that moment he began to dream of empire. He wished to make himself the interpreter of a new Napoleonic theory, which, it must be confessed, seemed elastic enough in character. According to his lights he came to repair and to fulfil; in fact, he posed as the redeemer of the great Emperor's dying pledges, the executor of his last will and testament. He lost no time in publishing his *Rêveries Politiques, Projets de Constitutions*, and several works of like calibre, which not only afford us some insight into his character, but also show that this youthful scion of the Imperial House had no intention that the Imperial name should sink into oblivion. All his literary compositions are saturated with the Napoleonic idea.

"L'Empereur n'est plus," he writes in 1839, "mais son esprit n'est pas mort. Privé de la possibilité de défendre par les armes son pouvoir tutelaire je puis au moins essayer de défendre sa memoir par des écrits. Éclairer l'opinion en recherchant la pensée qui a présidé à ses hautes conceptions, rappeler ses vastes projets est une tache qui sourit encore à mon cœur et qui me console de l'exile."

With the great example of his uncle thus ever

before him, he strove to follow in his footsteps and to emulate his greatness. His ambition never allowing him any respite, in the year 1836 he was ready to put his chances to the test, but his daring attempts only proved too premature. Appearing among the military at Strasburg, he had hoped to gain a footing on the ladder which was to reach to Empire, but he was overpowered and ignominiously shipped off to America by the Orleanist Government, which supplied him with money, and thought it superfluous to bring him to trial. In 1837, however, he was recalled to Europe by the news of his mother's last illness. On this occasion the French demanded his expulsion from Switzerland, thus showing that he had already gained the reputation of a dangerous adventurer, to be watched with due precaution; and so, with a somewhat doubtful prestige, he returned to England, where he led an incongruous life, dividing his time between society of low degree and the company of celebrities who met in the best-known London *salons*.

It was at this period that the chatterbox Greville met him, and subsequently left it on record that Louis Napoleon was a short, thickish, vulgar-looking man, without the slightest resemblance to his Imperial uncle, or any intelligence in his countenance! This also appears to have been the verdict of the majority who had then or subsequently the privilege of his acquaintance, but contemporary accounts vary considerably as to his manners and general deportment. He usually appeared quiet and constitutionally indolent, he was not easily excited, he was wont to be gay and humorous when at his ease. He disliked music. His general education seemed very deficient, even on subjects which ought to have been of the first necessity to him. For example, he was ignorant of the political history of modern times and political sciences generally; but he seemed remarkably honest in acknowledging these defects, and showed the greatest candour in admitting them. Nevertheless all that referred to Napoleonic history he seemed to have at his fingers'-ends, and his conversation left the impression that he had thought much and deeply on politics, although still an amateur in these matters, mixing many very sound and many very crude notions together. He never could have possessed an attractive character, but the mere fact that he was an Imperial wanderer would have been sufficient recommendation to Lady Blessington and others who delighted to bring together in their drawing-rooms a *mêlée* of artists, writers, musicians, and adventurers of all kinds, who made up in interest what they lacked in manners and personal attraction.

It is unnecessary further to enlarge upon this period of his life. Only half-acknowledged in London, he was as yet almost unknown except by name to his fellow-countrymen, and indeed it is said that so much of a stranger was he that he could not pronounce a sentence of French without a marked German accent. Desiring to force himself upon the French, in 1840 he made at Boulogne a second and equally abortive attempt upon France, with the result that he was condemned to perpetual imprisonment in the fortress of Ham, and became the laughing-stock of Europe. Yet this landing at Boulogne was only an egregious blunder in so far that it took the French nation by surprise, and he forgot that even the French nation is not so to be roused in cold blood.

But neither derision nor confinement leave effect upon such characters. The man who will attain his ends at all costs heeds not the smile of the pessimist. Louis Napoleon termed his confinement "a course of studies at the University of Ham," and in his prison he calmly continued his Bonapartist propaganda by writing *Aux Mânes de l'Empereur*. Engaged in these occupations, for five years he remained under watch and ward; but in 1846 he made good his escape and returned to England.

The revolution of 1848 naturally roused the would-be Emperor to further efforts. On the 10th of April in that memorable year Louis Napoleon was doing duty as a special constable in King Street, St James'. Possibly he wished to deceive those who charged him with ambition, but he must have made it clear that he would be prepared to fulfil any duty which the French people might lay upon him, and he doubtless saw once again a gleam of hope in the feverish state which seemed to infect like an epidemic every Government in Europe during that period of revolutions.

It has been said that the world at this time, intoxicated with the vision of boundless progress, pressed impatiently against the barriers erected by political systems which seemed to it worn-out and useless, and therefore intolerable. In France the spirit of revolt was not new-born. As early as 1843 the French were growing weary of the existing system, and there was a distinct resuscitation of what we may call the Napoleonic spirit in France. The steady maintenance of peace under the rule of Louis Philippe, which had proved distasteful to the ambitious, doubtless contributed to this in no small degree. In literature, too, Thiers and Béranger had recalled to mind the great exploits of the World Conqueror. Although to the casual onlooker, Louis Philippe seemed secure upon his throne, it was patent to those who understood this mood of the French that one gust of popular passion would be sufficient to overthrow the House of Orleans. From the restoration of the bronze statue on the top of the Vendôme column, in 1831, to the laying of the granite coffin beneath the dome of the Invalides, in 1840, France was being turned into one vast Napoleonic monument. The cry of "Vive la Reforme" was not unusual in the streets of Paris, but when to this was supplemented "À bas Guizot!" it was high time for the listless old monarch to bestir himself and to set about redressing the alleged grievances of his people.

The dismissal of the unpopular Minister, however, was not sufficient to satisfy the more ardent reformers who day by day were drifting towards fanatical Republicanism. By the end of the year 1847 matters had come to such a pass that the Socialist section of the community seemed likely to be in the ascendant. Early in the following year the worn-out sovereign was dinned out of his palace by the cries of a mob whose hatred for the existing *régime* was too violent to brook suppression. The seat of power was transferred from the Tuileries to the Hôtel de Ville, and Paris found herself divided by two parties, the one represented by the advocates of a purely political change, the other represented by the advocates of a thorough-going social revolution.

Paris, in fact, was in grave peril. The floodgates of Republicanism had been opened, and now the Liberals somewhat tardily awoke to the danger and set about stemming the tide which threatened to destroy every chance of a settled Constitution and the construction of a responsible Government. Luckily for the welfare of the citizens the Socialists found themselves in an insignificant minority when the elections to the New Assembly were published. A small affray in the streets of Paris proved sufficient to settle the matter, and order being restored, the Assembly was thenceforth free to draw up some form of a Constitution without fear of anarchy.

Now the French revolution of 1848 had in some measure been a victory of the workingmen, and since it was to this class that he had addressed especially some of his political theories, the circumstance encouraged Louis Napoleon to try his luck once again in his native country, and it was as the representative of these same working classes that he wished to take his seat in the Constituent Assembly of June; but after some consideration he resolved to return to England, as his election might have occasioned serious disputes. With great cunning he sent a notice from London to the National Assembly, in which he stated that "the hostile manner which the executive power had adopted towards him made it his duty to refuse a distinction which was said to have been gained by intrigue."

This well-calculated reserve increased the feeling in his favour, and brought about the effect that it was intended to produce. His quintuple election recalled him in September, and he thereupon commenced his candidature for the Presidency. The time had at last arrived for him to carry out his long-cherished plans, and on this occasion fortune was not to play him false. The times were propitious for introducing a change of some kind, but the country was not in the mood for a Socialist revolt; it was in an adventurous mood, and, being so, was ready to look to an adventurer to pull her through her difficulties. Persigny, one of Louis Napoleon's kindred spirits, declared that France was a democracy that needed discipline, and that no element was so fitted to represent it as the Napoleonic.

Possibly he was right. Whether his opinion was shared by the majority or not, at any rate France seemed to need a Napoleon, and there was now one at hand for her ready-made.

In November, 1848, the new Constitution was drawn up, based, it was alleged, upon the principle of the division of power, although in reality the great authority given to the President hindered the operation of such a principle, and left him the head of the army, the head of the bureaucracy, and in virtue of his election by the people endowed with powers co-ordinate with those of the legislature. Here at last was Louis Napoleon's opportunity, and he was not slow to recognise that the assumption of such powers would serve his purpose to carry out a policy which should ultimately secure him the imperial crown. After 1848, Louis Napoleon steps forward as the representative of order and authority, and as the declared enemy of Socialism. His victory, therefore, was welcomed as one over the Red Republicans. The French were pleased, and they did not fear mischief. They made two mistakes, M. Thiers said in after years, the first when they took him for a fool, the second when they took him for a genius, but it was not until the appearance of a letter to Colonel Ney, in which Louis Napoleon ostentatiously separated himself from his ministers, that suspicions of danger to the Republic from his ambition arose. In due course he was elected President with a large majority over his opponent Cavaignac, a sincere Republican; one who in his official acts and utterances spared the feelings of the reactionary classes as little as he spared those of the Socialists.

On the 20th of December he took the Oath of Allegiance to the Republic, binding himself to defend the Constitution of 1848. This oath declared every act of the President which dissolved the Assembly or prorogued it to be actually treason. "The oath which I have just taken," he said, "commends my future conduct. My duty is clear, I shall fulfil it as a man of honour. I shall regard as enemies of the country all those who endeavour to change by illegal means what all France has established." At the same time, he intimated that he accepted the candidature because three successive elections, and the unanimous decree of the National Assembly against the proscription of his family, warranted him in believing that France regarded the name he bore as one that might consolidate society which under the old *régime* had been shattered to its foundations.

For a few days concord seemed established between the different political parties in the Assembly, but early in the year 1849 a struggle

commenced between the President and the
majority of the members. Louis Napoleon took
all precautions. It was not his habit to admit
many persons to his confidence, but it was essential
for his success that there should be in each department some one to safeguard his interests. St.
Arnaud, a brilliant soldier, who had commanded
a brigade in Algiers, was made Minister of War
at the cost of many lives. It had even been
thought necessary to arrange a campaign to
bring this officer's name into sufficient prominence
to justify his ministerial appointment! The
command of the army in Paris had been given
to General Magnan, who had hinted that he was
ready to support Louis Napoleon in any venture.
An officer, pledged to keep the National Guard
in inaction, awaited further instructions. M. de
Maupas, a Préfet who sent to the President
reports which ought to have been sent to the
Ministers, now managed the police, and besides
these men there were others, such as Morny,
Persigny, and Fleury, who, although they were not
adapted to fill posts of responsibility in the State,
were sufficiently ambitious and devoid of public
morality to serve Louis Napoleon's purpose. He
himself continually paraded as a protector of
popular rights and of national prosperity, thus
carrying out in practice the theory that the

Napoleonic name was the symbol of order and security. Perceiving the flaw in the existing Napoleonic creed, he announced the coming not of the Cæsarian, but of the Augustine age.

Years before he had given to the world his interpretation of such a theory in the oft-quoted sentence:—" Les principes sur lesquels réposaient les lois impériales sont: l'égalitè civil d'accord avec les principes d'ordre et de stabilité. Napoléon est le chef suprême de l'état, l'élu du peuple, le représentation de la nation," and it was with this interpretation of the Napoleonic scheme of government that he now intended to win the hearts of the French people. As yet, however, the National Assembly seemed to hamper all his efforts to make his power perpetual. Accordingly, before the end of the year, he determined to throw off the mask, deeming that his plans were sufficiently well laid to admit of daring measures. Doubtless his judgment was on this occasion correct. Everything seemed to be in his favour. The power that he had recently acquired rested on universal suffrage, and it was independent of the Chamber. His large majority had clearly shown that the magic name had not lost its charm during the last thirty years, and finally, he had the army at his back, the army that had already greeted .n with shouts of " Vive l'Empereur." Louis

Napoleon made the most of these advantages, both with skill and with cunning. Nothing, however, reveals the baser side of his character so much as the methods he employed in winning over the army to his side. At first the generals had been for the most part Orleanists, or Republicans, and their sympathies doubtless permeated the ranks. Still even here there was a loophole for the President. As the generals of the highest position were hostile to the Bonapartists, nothing was easier than to tempt their subordinates with the prospect of their places. This corruption was so successful in its object that Changarnier was rendered helpless. Nor was this the only method by which Louis Napoleon sought to win back the affection of the army for his House. Military banquets were given in which the sergeant and the corporal sat side by side with the higher officers. Double rations of brandy, besides innumerable money bribes, were distributed to the garrison of Paris. A strange contrast it is, Napoleon I. appealing to the patriotic sense of the army, Napoleon III. appealing to their stomachs!

It had now become apparent that the Constitution of 1848 had proved hopelessly impracticable, for there were at this time two great powers in the State, each deriving its existence from the same source, each jealous of the other, without an umpire to decide in cases of disagreement. Above all, a fatuous provision of the Constitution decreed that the powers of the President and the Chamber were to terminate in 1852; a practical guarantee that anarchy and civil strife would be renewed on the expiration of the term of office. The admirers of Louis Napoleon never cease to lay stress upon the danger to which this provision would have exposed the French nation, and they maintain that under the circumstances his breach of faith can be plausibly condoned. Be this as it may, a message came from Louis Napoleon in October, 1849, to the Assembly, declaring that the victory which he had won in the previous December was a victory of the Napoleonic system which meant order, authority, religion, national prosperity within, national dignity without. In order therefore to save the Republic from anarchy, and to maintain the prestige of France among other nations he expressed his intention of substituting men of action for the present Ministers in office. Having delivered himself of his new plan, he proceeded to place in power men whose very insignificance guaranteed to him the influence which was needed to further his schemes. From this moment there grew up a party in the State composed of adventurers in all walks of life, who perceived that it was in their interest to exalt the Prince of Adventurers at the cost of parliamentary government.

There can be little doubt that at the time there was a general feeling existing all over France that this scheme would prove not only abortive but dangerous, and these fears were evinced in monster petitions demanding a revision of the Constitution. Louis Napoleon took the French at their word, declaring that the people should suffer no harm under his care, but in order that he might effect any change a majority of at least three-quarters was required, and unfortunately a majority of three-quarters was not to be obtained. In 1851, however, the refusal of the Comte de Chambord to sanction any appeal to the popular vote left the Assembly to choose between re-electing Louis Napoleon as President, or to run the risk of a *coup d'état*.

On the 19th of July the plan to revise the Constitution was rejected, so that Louis Napoleon, who could already accuse the Assembly of having destroyed universal suffrage, was now able to charge it with forbidding the nation to select its own head. This was all that he wanted to complete the groundwork of his plans, and he forthwith decided to carry out his *coup d'état*, but St Arnaud warned him not to take action until the winter. This advice was proffered for more than one very good reason. In the first place, if the arrest of all the leading men in Paris was to be contemplated such a move could only be attempted when the Assembly was sitting, and in the second place, the populace would be more likely to regard Louis Napoleon's cause as their cause if they saw him struggling for their rights in the Assembly itself. Louis Napoleon deemed that the time for action had arrived. He made his preparations with the utmost audacity, secrecy and adroitness, amusing his enemies meanwhile with the semblance of negotiations which he never intended seriously to fulfil, and relying upon the army by whose aid he had drawn together all power into his own hands. By his peremptory measures and arbitrary acts he showed that he was resolved to do nothing by halves. He gave confidence as to the stability of his future government, he raised his own reputation by his energy and ability, and he confirmed waverers in the belief that it was he alone who could save France at this critical juncture. But to realise the depth of immorality which Louis Napoleon reached it must be noticed that he made the refusal of the Assembly to repeal the electoral law of 31st of May the occasion of his *coup d'état*, although his own Ministers had overthrown universal suffrage. On his requiring that the repeal of the law of the 31st of May should be proposed, the Cabinet resigned, leaving the way open to St Arnaud and Maupas, and giving Louis Napoleon the opportunity that he required.

Before daybreak on the 2nd of December many of the most eminent statesmen in France were, by his orders, arrested in their beds and sent to prison, some of them afterwards even being exiled. On the previous evening Louis Napoleon had held a public reception at the Elysée. Before the guests dispersed he withdrew to his study to make final arrangements with the conspirators. At dead of night Maupas summoned his agents to the Préfecture of Police, charging each with their duties to arrest the leading men of Paris. Morny, the President's reputed half-brother and a man of an adventurous temperament like himself, was in the meanwhile engaged in telegraphing to the provinces to inform them with what joy Paris had hailed the change of government.

As a matter of fact Paris had not had the time or the liberty to ask herself whether she enjoyed the change or not. The Chamber had been occupied by soldiers, and its members had been placed in confinement. The High Court of Justice had been dissolved by force. Martial law had been proclaimed. Orders had been issued that those who resisted the usurpation in the streets were to be shot at once without trial. Desultory fighting in the boulevards had soon been put a stop to. All liberty of the press and of public meeting had been vetoed. The proclamations of Louis Napoleon, distributed sentence by sentence to different compositors, were set in type before the workmen knew upon what they were engaged. A Consultative Commission was announced and placarded in Paris, containing even the names of many who had refused to serve thereon in order to deceive the people into thinking that the President had a large following at his back.

Three proclamations had been issued. The first announced in the name of the French people that the National Assembly was dissolved and that universal suffrage was restored. The second denounced the monarchical conspirators within the Assembly, and also the anarchical elements therein. The third was a fervent appeal to the army. Every public functionary who had not given in his submission to the new government had been peremptorily dismissed, and the préfets had been given the power to send out to penal settlements any individual who belonged to a secret society; and through it all Louis Napoleon directed operations. He certainly was not deficient in cunning, and he could always play double with great conviction. While he reminded the army of the military glories of the first Empire, he declared to the people that the only conquests which he contemplated were those of commercial development in France. Under these conditions then Paris had been forced to say that she enjoyed the change, but she did so at the point of the bayonet.

It must at the same time be admitted that there is not much evidence to prove that the French people as a whole did offer any real objection to the President's actions, although the *coup d'état* did not pass off altogether without resistance. Barricades were erected in the streets as a matter of course, and on the 4th December divisions of the army converged from all directions upon the "insurgents." The troops lost some twenty-eight killed and a hundred and eighty wounded, but they succeeded in overcoming the mob. Not satisfied with their success they commenced indiscriminate firing on the boulevards with a consequent great loss of life, an estimate of which will never be obtained. Two thousand arrests followed, including that of Victor Hugo and that of Thiers. Resistance also was not absent in the rural districts, but these outbreaks only served the President's purpose. With characteristic ingenuity be represented these in glaring colours as the outbreaks of anarchism, from which he intended to save France.

Few of the people could really have approved of his very violent measures and arbitrary acts, but, on the other hand, there had been such a very general feeling of contempt for the existing Constitution, and of disgust at the conduct of the Assembly and the parties which divided it, that scarcely any lamented their overthrow, or regarded with the slightest interest or compassion the leaders who had been so brutally and ignominiously treated. Moreover, on such occasions the French are a people restless, fierce, and excitable, ever eager for change. At one moment they are seen acquiescing without a struggle in the impudent and vulgar rule of the "blackguards and mountebanks" of the provisional government; the next moment completely submitting themselves to the severe and unlimited military despotism of an adventurer. Thus then it came about that the second Napoleon had his Deux Décembre in the same way that the first Napoleon had his Dix-huit Brumaire.

Only a few weeks after the *coup d'état* the French nation had, by an appreciable majority declared itself in favour of a new Constitution in which the President should hold office for ten years, being assisted by a Ministry which should be responsible to him alone. Laws were to be prepared in a Council of State. The President had power to nominate members of the Senate, and in the Lower House he could nominate candidates agreeable to himself.

On the first day of the New Year Louis Napoleon attended a service of thanksgiving in Notre Dame Cathedral for the inestimable benefits that he had conferred upon his countrymen. On the same day he took possession of the Tuileries and restored the eagle as the military emblem of France. As he entered the royal palace Louis Napoleon must indeed have felt that there was nothing now to complete the imperial dignity but the name. Exactly a year afterwards he took upon himself the title of Emperor with the apparent acquiescence of the French nation.

It may be safely said that never in the history of the world has one man undertaken a task more utterly beyond the power of mortal man than that which Louis Napoleon was pledged to carry through. He professed to be at one and the same time the elect sovereign of the people, a son of the Revolution, a champion of universal suffrage, and an adversary of the demagogues. In the first of these characters he was bound to justify his elevation by economic and social reforms, in his second character he had to destroy the last trace of political liberty. He had, in fact, assumed various utterly incompatible attitudes, and the day that the masses found themselves deceived in their expectations, and the middle classes found their interests were betrayed, reaction was inevitable. For the present, however, all seemed to go smoothly. The leading European Powers were taken so much by surprise that they were unable to offer any effectual obstruction to the new turn of events in France. The majority perhaps were too much occupied with their own affairs to find the opportunity. True it is that the Czar Nicholas declined at first to acknowledge the full title of the French Emperor, and it seemed as if trouble was likely to emanate from this quarter, but in reality the hostile attitude of Russia only served Louis Napoleon's purpose. He was in fact bent on war from the first, for he knew that war could alone enhance the meagre prestige which at present was attaching to his name, and it was in the Crimean War that he saw the chances of gratifying his subjects by military glory. Already suspecting that the testimony of the plebiscite was deception, already believing that the people did not like him, nay, that they looked upon him with aversion, he embarked upon a war which would not only, he hoped, please the populace and the army, but would also make the name of Napoleon more real.

But it must be allowed that when he went to war he hoped for something more than mere military glory. He believed, that "no peace would be satisfactory that did not resuscitate Poland." With these two objects in view he joined the Allies in 1854.

It is not a little remarkable that the first enterprise of international importance, which France undertook after harbouring vengeance ever since the day of Waterloo, should have been planned in concert with the very country upon which vengeance for that defeat was to be wreaked.

Into the details of the Crimean War it is superfluous here to enter, it is only necessary to examine the effect of this European disturbance upon the power and prestige of Louis Napoleon. The latter, eager for an alliance with England, and above all things eager to play a great part before Europe himself, proposed that the combined fleets should pass the Bosphorus. It is the fate of all adventurers, if they wish to retain power, to retain it at the cost of blood, a price that can only be paid with great risk to their own integrity and to their popularity among their countrymen, and Louis Napoleon was no exception to the rule. It had been his grand design to come in person to the Crimea, to land with a fresh army on the south-eastern coast, to march across the interior of the peninsula, and to complete the investment of Sebastopol from the north; thus to end by one grand stroke the war which the allied forces seemed to be unable to complete. This scheme sounded magnificent, but unfortunately Canrobert was bound to help Lord Raglan, who was investing Sebastopol from the south. When therefore Louis Napoleon ordered the recall of the soldiers for his own purposes, Canrobert resigned. Pelissier took his place, but he, too, flatly refused to obey the Emperor's orders, so that any hopes that Louis Napoleon may have entertained of playing a prominent part during the actual hostilities in the Crimea were dashed to the ground. After the war at the Conference of Paris; as the champion of the principal of nationality against the Treaties of 1815, he proposed that the provinces of Moldavia and Wallachia, while remaining in dependence on the Sultan, should be united into a single State under a prince chosen by themselves; but the English Ministry would not hear of such a union.

Nevertheless, although the advice of Louis Napoleon had not been uniformly adopted, there can be no question that the war enhanced his prestige at home. Undoubtedly before the

Crimean War his position had been extremely precarious. The coldness with which foreign sovereigns had met his proposals of marriage forms one of the many proofs that no one entertained the idea that his power was lasting. The part which he had recently played in European affairs changed all this, and there now seemed every prospect that he would be recognised as the genuine ruler. He could, under these circumstances, make his voice heard in the great conferences of European Powers, and France could again take her place among the nations.

Those were the palmy days of the second Empire. Besides the authority which he had acquired by a successful foreign policy, Louis Napoleon had thoroughly gauged the French character, and he knew well that vanity was the nation's weakness, to flatter which was one of the surest ways of maintaining his power; and although in his private life he preferred almost bourgeois simplicity, no effort was too great, no ceremony too striking or theatrical when he appeared as Emperor. With the aid of an inordinately extravagant wife he maintained a Court, which in all its gaudiness and splendour rivalled the traditions of the ancient royal house of France. Fabulous magnificence was displayed whenever foreign sovereigns came as guests to the Imperial palace, whither they proceeded in large numbers, from Queen Victoria to the dusky Queen of Madagascar. The Emperor sought by all the means within his power to preserve the Napoleonic traditions, and to lull the Parisians into sweet dreams, as if the glorious days of Napoleon the Great had returned. Thus at the conclusion of peace he seemed to have reached the zenith of his ambitions. The birth of the Prince Imperial at this time seemed to add the finishing touch to his good fortune; but with all this apparent prosperity he interpreted the French character too well to feel really secure upon his throne.

It was his conviction that one of the most important lessons to be learnt from history is that a dynasty has only the chance of existing if it remains loyal to its origin and protects the public interests for which it was founded. If once the people of Paris conceived the notion that every act of the Emperor was not for the public good, he knew that his overthrow was but a question of time.

For the present in France there seemed to be sincere faith in the undisputed though pacific ascendency of the Empire over the council of the nations, in the necessity for the revision of ancient treaties, for a re-modelling of the map of Europe, for the emancipation of enslaved nations, and for the protection of minor States. But the popularity of the Emperor himself had not increased. It was noticed on all sides, as early as the year 1858, that he had grown insouciant, indolent and utterly careless of the effect he produced, at all events among the upper classes, although he still curried favour with the mob. The Emperor's personal character was a fruitful topic of conversation among all ranks of Paris Society, and, thanks to those who faithfully kept journals during this period, some of the opinions of those who were best qualified to give them have been preserved. Not the least interesting is a certain passage in the diary of an English diplomat who has recorded an interview he obtained with Mons. Drouyn de Lluys, some time Foreign Minister, which it is as well to reproduce verbatim. " My *scéance* with Mons. Lluys concluded with a very detailed and interesting analysis of the Emperor's character. 'You do not,' said he, 'possess the ordinary means of forming an estimate of his designs and intentions that the character of most men permit you with. He is neither governed by passions nor principles. Whereas most men desire to mould circumstances to their own views, he is content to await events and mould his views and designs to circumstances according as they turn up. He is more guided by his character and constitution than his intellect. *C'est la cervelle plûtot que l'intelligence qui le dirige,* but he has the inestimable advantage of having a sangfroid imperturbable, *rien ne le demente.* He is like a moderate whist-player, plying his adversaries with champagne. Although these adversaries are far superior to him when sober, he has the best of them when they are drunk. Or again, to adopt a fishing simile, *Il aime pêcher en eau trouble. Il ne pêche pas bien, mais il peut voir le poisson dans l'eau trouble et par consequent le prendre, tandis que les pêcheurs qui lui sont bien superieurs ne le voient même pas.* That is why he always likes *confusion dans les affairs.* He is cool and collected while every one else loses their heads, and the result is that by hook or by crook he gets his own way when far abler men fail. He listens to what you say, even seems to acknowledge that you are right, yet acts directly in the teeth of your advice without any apparent motive or being able to account for the impulse he yielded to. In this he is like a man who commits a causeless murder, and as answer to the judge questioning him as to what could have driven him to the crime says—*Dame! Mons. le President, c'est une idée qui m'est venu.* He is very fond of astonishing people. This is very often the reason of his doing things apparently unaccountable. He has a childish enjoyment of the affected *ébahissement* and lifting up of hands of the *entourage*. There are some people who are fond of admiration and at the same time of glory, and it is these who do really great things, but he is only fond of that lower species of admiration which is extorted by actions in themselves leading to no beneficial result, but which dazzle by their magnitude. He is also actuated by a strong desire, being as he said himself, a parvenu, to destroy as much as he can all associations in men's minds with old dynasties, and this has much to do with the gigantic works he has undertaken in Paris, and which are carried on much more for the sake of obliterating the past and modernising than improving the town." This lively character study may serve to throw fresh light upon the Emperor's motives and behaviour. It is certain, at any rate, that he was rapidly losing the confidence of all the best men in France, and that he was now becoming so self-concentrated and so distrustful of his Ministers that none but men who had forfeited their independence of character would consent to serve him.

On the 14th of January, 1858, Felice Orsini tried to assassinate Louis Napoleon, and failed. The miscreant threw a bomb under the carriage which was conveying the Emperor and Empress to the opera, but no explosion took place. It was noticed that not a cheer greeted the Sovereigns when they took their places in the theatre, although what had occurred in the streets was immediately known in the building. This attempt on the Emperor's life was to have far-reaching consequences. At first he was disposed to regard as dilatory the subsequent behaviour of the Sardinian Government, but Orsini's dying prayer, "Free my country and the blessings of twenty-five million Italians will go with you," had doubtless eaten its way into the Emperor's romantic imagination, and it is not too much to say that he was encouraged to the campaign in Lombardy by the murderous attack of Orsini on his own person. So it came about that in the year 1859 the restless ambition of the Emperor found scope in a war against Austria on behalf of Italian unity. Cavour had supported Louis Napoleon throughout his controversy with England and Austria on the settlement of the Danubian Principalities, not, of course, without hope of reciprocal advantage, and the time had now arrived for Louis Napoleon to return the compliment, but we must not deny to him a very genuine, if not profound sympathy with the Italian national cause. Moreover, it must be remembered that if he was to be the chief exponent of the principle of nationality, the best way to set about convincing Europe upon the subject would be for him to drive the Austrians out of Italy.

Accordingly, at the customary reception of ambassadors on New Year's Day he observed with regret that the relations of the two empires were not so satisfactory as they had been, and in May of the same year, playing for once into the hands of the Republicans, he made the famous remark that Italy should be free from the Alps to the Adriatic. With this giant project in view he proceeded to form an alliance with Victor Emmanuel who, guided by Cavour, was eager to place himself at the head of the Italian national party. Louis Napoleon held a personal interview with Cavour at Plombières, but the French Ministers were, as usual, kept in the dark. It flattered Louis Napoleon's *amour propre* to take into secret partnership a man whose place in history he divined. "There are only three men in Europe," was his famous remark to Cavour, "we two, and then a third whom I will not name."

In February a pamphlet was published in Paris which revealed the plans of the Emperor. For the purpose of satisfying the nationalist feeling and of saving the Pope from an impossible position, it declared that the disturbed condition of Italy made a change in the government imperative. A scheme of federation seemed to be the obvious remedy, but since Austria would be certain to offer objections to any such proposal the only course that remained was to expel Austria from Italy. In February Louis Napoleon had seemed determined upon war, but in March he began to waver in his resolution. There was certainly need for reflection. We may blame Louis Napoleon for his vacillation, but it must be allowed that in this instance he was taking a very risky course. The Crimean War, which had proved beneficial to his own position, had intoxicated him, and at first he could see nothing but advantage to himself in a fresh attack upon the Treaties of 1815 which would weaken the House of Austria, still regarded as the hereditary enemy of France, and in the expulsion of the Austrian army from Northern Italy, where its presence offended the populations; but except the Republicans who hailed a policy likely to bring about a return to the old traditions of Freedom and Nationality, nobody in France was able to perceive the benefit likely to accrue from such an undertaking. He was embarking therefore upon a war of no obvious necessity, against the sentiment of his own country. A stronger man under such circumstances might well have hesitated. The English Government was endeavouring to interfere with offers of mediation, the other European Powers were not to be trusted, and yet Victor Emmanuel was threatening to abdicate and leave Italy to her own resources if the Emperor of the French did not abide by his previous determination.

In March, Louis Napoleon suddenly proposed that the Italian question should be laid before a Congress of Powers, but Austria would only consent to this proposal on the understanding that Piedmont would disarm. In April an ultimatum reached Turin from Vienna, threatening invasion if this demand was not complied with. Louis Napoleon thereupon judged that the time for a decided policy had arrived, and he accordingly declared war. Although we may give him the credit for having at heart the welfare of Italy, still he doubtless took into consideration that the ejection of Austria might be the occasion of a bond of alliance between the freed nation and its deliverer; a bond which could afterwards be strengthened into a compact of indirect allegiance. At any rate he had now made up his mind on a course of action, and taking the command of his army in person he marched to the front.

Success attended his progress, and after the

victory of Magenta, which was looked upon as a triumph for the French arms, the allies entered Milan on the 8th of June. Soon afterwards the hard-fought battle of Solferino finally shattered the hopes of the Austrians. There exists some proof that Louis Napoleon was thinking of peace the day before that battle, which goes far to dispose of the story that he changed his mind under the impression left on him by the scene of carnage. It was probably a reason less sentimental in character that made him ponder. Although the game seemed now in his hands, in reality he was not overjoyed at a success which seemed to redound too much to the credit of the Italians.

He realised that a recently united and ambitious people would soon learn to resent the patronage of France, and being on the frontier would only prove a source of trouble and anxiety to the French Government. But apart from these considerations it was only to be expected that the other European Powers, with the exploits of Napoleon I. ever fresh in their memory, would resent all the attempts of the new Emperor to follow in his footsteps. The Prussian troops had even been mobilised against such a contingency, and there were rumours in the air of a defensive federation of Europe. In the face of these facts there seemed every prospect of peace. Nor was Louis Napoleon averse to such a conclusion. It must always be remembered that he hated the noise of war, not by any means because he was deficient in physical courage, but because there was that in his disposition which made him turn in horror from the sight of suffering and bloodshed. In after years the very mention of the names Magenta and Solferino caused him to shudder. Desirous then of peace he turned to England.

Now Palmerston's friendliness towards Louis Napoleon had, in recent years, somewhat cooled, and at the present crisis he was one of the many who wished to see Italy erected into a strong kingdom, capable of resisting the advances of both Austria and France. Seeing therefore little prospect of gaining any assistance in this quarter, Louis Napoleon turned to Austria, and negotiations with the Emperor Francis Joseph resulted in the armistice of Villafranca. The terms arranged at their meeting were these.

The Emperor of Austria was not to cede any part of Venetia, but he gave up Lombardy and consented to the establishment of an Italian federation under the Presidency of the Pope. At the same time he insisted that Mantua should remain within his own frontier, and that the sovereigns of Tuscany and Modena should resume possession of their dominions. That Louis Napoleon should assent to these terms was an act of political necessity, but, of course, under the circumstances, public opinion ascribed his assent to treachery or pusillanimity. The truth of the matter was that Louis Napoleon was attempting something Napoleonic, in other words, something beyond his powers. His dream had been to erect a kingdom of Central Italy, the crown of which was to be worn by his cousin, Prince Napoleon, the son-in-law of Victor Emmanuel, but the development of popular feeling during the war had soon proved to him that such aspirations were futile. The present situation revealed the weakness in his character, and seriously damaged his reputation for moral courage. He could decide on no policy but that of forbidding the annexation of the Central States to Piedmont, although after the peace of Zurich he again had recourse to the same Napoleonic method which had helped him out of the wood more than once before.

If Italy was to become a consolidated nation, the cession of Savoy and Nice to France must be the price paid for compensation; but this could not be effected without the reversal of his former policy. Never was there worse policy, it has been truly said, than that of helping to free Italy, and then deliberately rooting out gratitude from her heart.

Now, although the European Powers in Congress had consented to settle the Italian question they would do so only on the condition that the French frontier was not extended. At the last moment Louis Napoleon determined deliberately to wreck the schemes that he had previously formulated, and he thereupon resorted to a clever ruse by issuing a manifesto which effectually enraged the Austrian Government and hindered all chance of a peaceful settlement in Congress.

On the 24th of December, 1859, at the instigation of Louis Napoleon a pamphlet was published, entitled *The Pope and the Congress.* The doctrine of this essay was briefly, that Rome and the territory immediately around it, if guaranteed to the Pope by the Great Powers, should be sufficient for the temporal needs of the Holy See. There followed upon this publication a battle royal between the French Emperor and the Holy Father. The outcome of it all was that the opposition of the latter gave Louis Napoleon a very good excuse for postponing the suggested Congress. On the 5th of January, 1860, the change in Louis Napoleon's policy was made evident to the world by the dismissal of his Foreign Minister, Walewski, and the appointment in his place of Thouvenel, a friend to Italian Unity.

The annexation of Nice and Savoy by the Emperor, which had been agreed upon at Plombières, was regarded as his first active movement towards the extension of the French frontier; a scheme which he was known to have at heart, and against which all Europe would thenceforth feel bound to take active precautions. Louis Napoleon complained that he was grossly misunderstood, and that no one ever gave him credit for the sincerity of his actions, but seeing that it was a case of "once bit twice shy" with his neighbours he was obliged to accept the situation. His argument, which sounds plausible enough, was that if Northern and Central Italy were to be fused into one kingdom, nothing was more natural than that his frontier should be a little better protected on that side, and that it was unfair to call the annexation of a small mountainous district to France by the name of a conquest or aggrandisement; it would be nothing but a measure of legitimate defence. On no other ground could the cession of Nice and Savoy be condemned than that this transfer was an indication that Louis Napoleon would not be content

I.]   THE CESSION OF NICE AND SAVOY   47

with the frontiers of 1815. The argument of the English Government, on the other hand, which could boast of just as much logic if not more, was that it was not so much the annexation of Savoy to France which caused the distrust that had been manifested on the subject, but the way in which it had been brought forward in spite of all Louis Napoleon's declarations in going to war. "People who knew nothing of His Majesty personally" Lord Cowley at the time commented, "could only judge by his acts, and those acts tended to create alarm." The English Ambassador told one of his colleagues that the Emperor had no deliberate intention of deceiving, and that he always intended to act up to his promises at the time they were made. When, however, circumstances changed, he believed he had a right to change also, and was much surprised at people not thinking that this was natural.

The fact of the whole matter was this. Louis Napoleon had been inconsistent and had not kept his word, with the result that this latter day Machiavellism was not working so smoothly as its author had designed. He thought that the cession of Nice and Savoy showed submission, but he was to be deceived once again. Even Lord Palmerston, who had been the Emperor's champion on previous occasions, and who had watched with delight the triumph of the Italian cause, was now enraged at the subtle intrigues of his erstwhile friend. Louis Napoleon was more than suspected of the intention of invading England, but the panic had subsided as soon as it became obvious that it was to the Emperor's interest to be on friendly terms with that country. He himself knew full well that a war with England, while it would have been without the shadow of a pretext, was an undertaking too formidable to be risked for the indulgence of personal aims with which the French nation did not sympathise, and which would have been disastrous to the growing commerce and flourishing industries which it was his steady aim to encourage and develop. It is interesting to conjecture what actually were the aims and ambitions of Louis Napoleon at this period. He must have long ago abandoned the hope of emulating his great predecessor. Whatever his aims may have been at first, henceforward fortune seemed to forsake him.

Up to the year 1860, the Empire remained absolute, but after the Italian war and the treaties of commerce it was committed to Liberalism and self-destruction. The prestige of the Emperor depended upon the success of the French arms, and so far French arms had fulfilled these conditions. He had helped to defeat Russia in the Crimea, and he had crushed the power of Austria in Italy, but his designs for further triumph in Europe were frustrated during the Polish rising of 1863. In that year the Poles had at last tried to obtain their independence. This disturbance only afforded Bismarck the opportunity of breaking up the *entente* between France and Russia, substituting a close alliance between the Czar and Germany, an arrangement which came as a great blow to Louis Napoleon, and which marks the beginning of his decline. Once again he was to experience the inconvenience and danger of double dealing, but when we accuse him of inconsistent policy we must remember the one great hindrance in his path. He could not venture to be unpopular. He feared unpopularity, and therefore he could not govern. He essayed to please all parties, and in the attempt pleased none. On this occasion he sent a formal note to St Petersburg to complain that Russia had broken the terms of the Treaty of Vienna, but the new *rôle* of Louis Napoleon as champion of the treaties was somewhat of a surprise to Europe, and perhaps it was not unnatural distrust of his sincerity that led Austria to reject his argument.

Although there was a short-lived alliance between Austria, England, and France, the

Poles were virtually left alone, and the revolt was quelled in a war almost unparaleled for its barbarity and ruthless massacre. The part that Louis Napoleon played in the Polish affair was indeed a sorry one, for he had not only offended Russia, but he had also laid himself open to the contemptuous derision of the whole of Europe, and of his own countrymen.

During the Schleswig-Holstein difficulty Louis Napoleon was able to retaliate upon England for refusing to support his plan for a European Congress by declining to allow the French to take up arms in conjunction with England. He told the English Government that the cause of Schleswig-Holstein to some extent represented the principle of nationality to which France was friendly, and that of all wars in which France could engage, a war with Germany would be the least desirable.

In September 1865 Bismarck was obliged to ask Louis Napoleon's assistance for the union of Italy and Russia against Austria, and with this object he interviewed the French Emperor at Biarritz; but, since there were no witnesses present, the precise nature of their conversation will never be known. That Louis Napoleon was now scheming for an extension of France on the north-east there can be little doubt, but in 1866 during the Austrian War it became evident that he had lost all control over events, and all chance of gaining the Rhenish provinces. Perhaps he had trusted too much to the "irresistible logic of events." His neighbours had moved too quickly for him. Germany achieved her union in 1866, and France came in too late for her share of the spoil. It would have been impolitic for Louis Napoleon at that time to ally himself with Austria against his own creation, the Italian kingdom, and again, he had no means of extorting cessions from Prussia when once Prussia was sure of an ally who could bring two hundred thousand men into the field. The neutrality of Louis Napoleon was not of his own choosing, nor could France now attach any credit to herself for this apparent disinterestedness on her part. After the battle of Sadowa the Austrian Emperor, who ceded Venetia to him on behalf of Italy, applied to Louis Napoleon for his mediation, which was accepted in principal by the King of Prussia. When these complicated negotiations were in progress Louis Napoleon at first fondly imagined that he had outwitted Bismarck by confining the Prussian Federation to the north of the Maine, and by securing in the Treaty the independence of the Southern States, but he soon realised that, far from being cut into two halves, a part of

Germany was consolidated, and Bismarck had kept the way open for the later extension of this union to the Southern States.

It was not only in Europe that Louis Napoleon had tried political experiments. The establishment of two powerful nations on his immediate frontier had turned his thoughts to the consideration of enhancing his prestige at home by means of extending his influence beyond the Atlantic. With this object he deliberately defied the Monroe Doctrine. In other words, he conceived a plan for the exaltation of the Latin races on the American Continent. Some years before England, France and Spain had protested against the decision of the Mexican Congress to suspend all payment to foreign creditors for two years. When European troops had landed the President yielded, and a convention was signed, but a message arrived from Louis Napoleon to the effect that he was willing to recognise the invitation which had been sent by certain Mexicans to the Archduke Maximilian of Austria to assume the Imperial dignity, and that he would support him by force if elected Emperor, in spite of the fact that the Powers on landing troops had disclaimed any intention of interfering with the internal affairs of the country.

This action of the Emperor broke up the

Triple Alliance; but the French persevered notwithstanding. Then followed one of the most melancholy and sordid episodes in the history of his reign. The Archduke, trusting to the assistance which the Emperor was unable in reality to give him, landed at Vera Cruz, and there found to his cost that the Monroe Doctrine was not to be defied with impunity. The American Civil War was now at an end, and there were troops in great numbers waiting in readiness to hold their own against the interloper. The United States moreover demanded the withdrawal of the French from Mexico. Louis Napoleon, driven into a corner by his own improvident ambitions, perforce consented, and left the wretched Maximilian to his fate.

The Empress Charlotte thereupon hastened to Europe, bearing with her the very letters in which the French Emperor had promised not to abandon her husband in his need, and forced him to read them through himself, while she knelt in the dust at his feet. But it was too late, he could do nothing to help her. He must indeed have felt that the glory of his imperial dignity had been tarnished. He had already been made the sport of European Powers, and now he had failed ignominiously to win laurels beyond the Atlantic. The only course that remained open to him was to advise Maximilian to abdicate, but the latter refused to adopt such a course, and in June of the year 1867 he met his death at the hands of the soldiers; the scapegoat of the Emperor's iniquity.

The fate of Maximilian naturally excited the compassion and anger of Europe; compassion for the unfortunate man who had been lured by specious promises into a veritable death-trap; anger against the gambler of fortune who, unable to keep his word, had deserted a kinsman in the hour of peril. Retribution was not far ahead. Storm-clouds were gathering thick and fast to eclipse the already fading glories of the Empire, and the hopes and aspirations of Louis Napoleon were being dissipated in rapid succession. His one ambition had been to place himself in an exalted position as the President of a great European Confederation that should include every nation constituted as a democratic community, bound by ties of gratitude to himself. Instead of such a coalition of friendly states under his presidency, Louis Napoleon found himself beset on every frontier by the menacing attitude of his neighbours. Worst of all the French people had taken alarm when they saw the consolidation of Prussia, and they were now determined at all costs to prevent the unification of Germany.

THE QUESTION OF LUXEMBOURG IN 1867

War seemed inevitable, for it was in war alone that Bismarck saw the chance of welding together the German Empire. Louis Napoleon had demanded under serious threats compensation for France on the left bank of the Rhine, a demand which was substituted, on Bismarck's refusal to yield a foot of German territory, by a demand for the cession of Luxembourg. When in 1867, relying on the support of Prussia, the Emperor had attempted to acquire Luxembourg, he had entered into negotiations with the King of Holland, who agreed to surrender the Duchy, on condition the Emperor should secure the assent of Prussia. Bismarck, at the last moment, played Louis Napoleon false by declaring that war would be the consequence, and by publishing the secret treaties with the Southern States. For the second time Louis Napoleon found himself duped and outwitted by the German diplomatist. The terms of the French Emperor had raised a storm of indignation in Germany, and this suited Bismarck's purpose, but as yet he was loth to declare war until he could make use of a more convincing pretext than the French claim to Luxembourg.

War, however, was inevitable. It seemed to be the fate of Louis Napoleon to draw his sword against his will. "L'idée napolonienne," he once wrote, "n'est point une idée de guerre, mais une idée sociale, industrielle, commercielle, humanitaire. Si pour quelques hommes il apparait toujours entourée de la foudre des combats c'est qu'elle fut en effet trop longtemps enveloppée par la fumée du canon et la poussière des batailles. Mais aujourd'hui les nuages sont dissipés et on entrerait à travers la gloire des armes une gloire civile plus grande et plus durable." All these hopes of consolidating his power on the strength of internal prosperity had now vanished, and there seemed nothing left but the fatal alternative of war. "L'Empire c'est la paix," could no longer be the maxim of Louis Napoleon while it was necessary to conciliate the army and to gratify the craving susceptibility of the French people. His main difficulty lay between conceding too much or too little to the war-like and domineering spirit of his subjects.

In the autumn of the year 1867 matters seemed nearing a crisis. Protracted negotiations with both Austria and Italy failed to elicit any substantial aid for France in her hour of peril, so that the Emperor's object now was, if not to gain allies, at any rate to gain time. Both attempts proved fruitless. France was to reveal her unprepared condition at the same time that she was to widen and complete her isolation. Louis Napoleon might set himself to soothe, to reassure the French people, but the "black spots on the horizon" were visible to all. He could not estimate French opinion because he had deprived the French of free utterance. To him, therefore, the assurance of almost boundless popular support was a source of weakness no less than of strength. On the other hand, Prussia was well prepared for all emergencies, and was only waiting for a plausible pretext to commence active hostilities. This was not difficult to find.

In September of the year 1868 Isabella had been driven off the throne of Spain, and had sought refuge at the French Court. On the 3rd of July 1870, the revolutionists offered the crown to Prince Leopold of Hohenzollern-Sigmaringen, who accepted their invitation; but the French people, mad with rage that a Hohenzollern should wear the crown of Spain, cried out that no Prussian prince should be their neighbour. The Duc de Grammont declared that in the event of such a contingency the French people would know how to do their duty without hesitation and without weakness, an utterance that Bismarck chose to construe as a threat of war. The King of Prussia, residing at the time in Ems, refused to interfere with the Prince of Hohenzollern's decision, but the latter nevertheless resigned in the interest of the peace of Europe. As a matter of fact his action only precipitated war, for the people of Paris were thirsting for revenge upon the hated Prussians. On the 13th of July the publication of the celebrated Ems telegram in Paris decided the matter, and in the evening war was declared. Louis Napoleon had postponed the evil hour as long as it was possible for him to do so. He had tried by the introduction of liberal institutions to free himself from the burden of government and the weight of responsibility which he had voluntarily taken upon himself; but, to quote the words of M. Thiers, "the successes which had once been matters of congratulation were now crowding their consequences upon him." When his ideas of a new Constitution were made known, people realised that he was graciously making a gift of what was already slipping through his fingers.

In September of 1869 Louis Napoleon in despair had recourse to the fatal expedient of so altering the Constitution that he virtually disavowed the principles which he had once declared to be essential to the government of the country, thus making a public and radical confession of weakness and error. His public acts were now full of hesitations and contradictions. Already the turbulent democracy had discovered a martyr in Baudin, one of the victims of the *coup d'état*. Radical and Republican pamphleteers gloated over the fatal illness which had now seized upon him, in language that outraged decency and humanity. There seemed only one course open to the unfortunate man, to give way to the hysteria of the Paris mob and the solicitations of the Empress Eugénie, who, seeing in a successful war the one chance of preserving the throne for her son, had represented to her husband that it was inevitable if the honour of France was not to become a mere empty phrase. Louis Napoleon cultivated an impassive exterior, but in reality his character was emotional, and like all emotional persons, he was susceptible to the magnetism of a stronger brain and will. The reputation of the Empress will doubtless suffer much at the hands of future historians for the part she played in this crisis of French history, but it is only fair to believe that for whatever she did amiss the tragedy of her declining years has fully atoned.

In making his final decision Louis Napoleon depended on the complete efficiency of the French army, and the co-operation of former friendly Powers. As a matter of fact the army was totally unprepared. The contractors were defrauding the Government; want and disorder characterised every department. Of the French army and the French military organisation at this time, it is impossible to speak with moderation. It was not that the soldiers were defective in courage, but that the Imperial Government was rotten to the core. The idea of a prompt inroad into Southern Germany was abandoned for the very good reason that besides defective transport there was a remarkable absence of whole regiments that figured in the order of battle. " The deficiencies of the army were made worse by the diversion of public funds to private necessities; the looseness, the vulgar splendour, the base standards of judgment of the Imperial Court had infected each branch of the public services of France, and worked perhaps not least on those who were in military command." The German army, on the other hand, owed its strength and organisation to a firm and upright government. In the face of these facts then what conclusions must we come to? Will the unbiassed judgment of posterity allow to Louis Napoleon some extenuating circumstances, or will it pronounce an unqualified condemnation upon the man who, for the sake of consolidating his own power and strengthening his corrupt Government, spilled the blood of no less than a hundred thousand Frenchmen?

The Emperor was now looked upon with suspicion in France. The Empire, to quote the words of a well-known writer, was being wrecked by the self contradictions of its origin, not having known how to find an equilibrium between the Conservative prejudices, which it had used for its own ends, and the revolutionary passion to which it owed its birth.

The democratic M. de Rochefort had done much to poison the minds of the French people against the Emperor in the columns of his scandalous paper the *Lanterne*. The errors that Louis Napoleon had committed in foreign negotiations had not contributed towards raising him in the estimation of his subjects, and finally he was attacked by a mortal disease, which effectually quenched all the fire and vigour of former days. Nevertheless, when war was declared, he took the command of the army in person, believing himself, as he always had done, to be possessed of the qualities of a great general as well as a great statesman. Aware of the numerical inferiority of his own troops, he hoped by extreme rapidity of movement to penetrate Southern Germany, before the Prussian army could assemble, and so, while forcing the Southern Governments to neutrality, to meet on the Upper Danube the assisting forces of Italy and Austria. It was his design to concentrate a hundred and fifty thousand men at Metz, a hundred thousand at Strasburg, and with these armies united to cross the Rhine into Baden; while a third army, which was to assemble at Chalons, protected the north-eastern frontier against an advance of the Prussians. He was, however, never able to cross the Rhine, and he was obliged to fight at great disadvantage within Alsace and Lorraine. The campaign opened with a small success at Saarbrücken, which the Emperor in his despatch magnified into a victory, but in the same month he suffered successive defeats at Weissenberg, Worth, and Spicheren. He then retired on Metz, leaving the chief command to Marshal Bazaine whose escape from that town was prevented by the successive defeats of Mars-la-Tour and Gravelotte. Metz surrendered in October.

Meanwhile a hastily organised force of one hundred and twenty thousand men under Macmahon, was moved to the assistance of Bazaine. On reaching Sedan, Macmahon found himself surrounded by the Germans, and suffered a crushing defeat. "The army is defeated and taken. I am a prisoner." So ran the curt telegram that Eugénie received in Paris announcing the virtual downfall of the Empire, and the overthrow of her ambitions.

Louis Napoleon had vainly sought death on the field of battle, drawing in rein and awaiting it amid a veritable shower of bullets to no purpose.

A capricious fate had yet in store for him two years of melancholy exile. Until the conclusion of peace he was confined at Wilhelmshohe, but, in March 1871, he was set at liberty and joined the Empress in England, whither she had escaped with difficulty after receiving the news of her husband's defeat at Sedan. He resided with her for a brief season at Chislehurst, weighed down with illness and affliction, until the 9th of January 1873, when he passed away without a sound, without a parting word.

In many respects we may say, that Louis Napoleon is one of the most pathetic figures in history, although to apply such an adjective to the name Napoleon sounds very like a contradiction in terms. Yet a cursory study of the chief events in his career will justify its use. Destitute of the abilities and of the education which are indispensable to a statesman, while seeking to be revered as the arbiter of Europe, he was forced to undergo all the humiliation and mortification which invariably fall to the lot of ambitious upstarts. Possessed of neither the virtues nor the vices which enable men to maintain greatness long, he was not afforded the time nor the opportunity to mature his schemes, with the result that he has left behind him no service rendered to mankind of sufficient importance to sanctify the means that he employed for his ends, and consequently few have given him credit for the good qualities which he really possessed. Aspiring to emulate in all respects his great predecessor he has forced posterity to institute a parallel between himself and Napoleon I., a comparison which applies with a peculiar infelicity to himself. Giving to the world at the outset of his career an example almost unrivalled in history of what endurance and resolution can effect against the greatest superiority of power, and spite of fortune, he failed to fulfil the expectations of his followers. He showed instead, a great want of judgment and self-command at several important crises, and in his later years gave proof to the world that neither his principles nor his spirit were such as could be trusted when strong temptations were to be resisted or serious dangers were to be braved.

Yet although we admit that Louis Napoleon is an object of pity he does not at the same time merit the scorn with which many of his critics have thought fit to stigmatise his name. Although it is impossible to criticise him without some expression of contempt, it is equally impossible to deny that he possessed many of those qualities which distinguish the great men of this world from the mean.

It is comparatively easy in dealing with the

career of any man, in whatever walk of life he may be, to make either a hero or a villain of him; but Louis Napoleon is an exception to the general rule. He was neither a hero nor a villain. If he had been either a more honest man or a more consistent knave he would have acquired a greater reputation for wisdom, and he would have earned a greater measure of admiration from his contemporaries and from posterity.

It is a melancholy truth, that if crimes are only committed on sufficiently large a scale, the perpetrator will often be more admired than blamed. Lord Macaulay once wrote that history after all is made up of the bad actions of extraordinary men. All the most noted destroyers and deceivers of our species, all the founders of arbitrary governments have been extraordinary men; in fact nine-tenths of the calamities which have befallen the human race have had no other origin than the union of high intelligence and low ideas.

Why is it that we reverence the name of Napoleon I. as one of the greatest in the whole history of the world? Was not his greatness and his influence the result of crimes committed on the most extensive scale? Did ever any one man exist before or since who has brought so much suffering into the world with so little compensation? Yet every generation of mankind adds a never decreasing tribute to his honour. It was by his great intelligence that he rose to such heights of earthly glory. But what other object influenced him but the ambition to make himself the greatest of our human race? Was there any other *arrière pensée* working in his mind, or were all his deeds actuated by the most undiluted selfishness? Without doubt it was low ideas that influenced him in all his actions, and it was the union of high intelligence and low ideas that enabled him to effect those great results which have made his name for all time one of the most sublime in history.

But if crimes are to call for admiration they must be upon the largest scale. It is magnitude that the human race invariably admires. To take the simplest and most obvious instance of this truth there are many buildings which are considered among the most impressive and the most awe-inspiring in the world which, if they had been planned upon a smaller scale, would appear to us meagre and insignificant. It is so too with the misdeeds of mankind. The wretch who steals his neighbour's watch is merely despised and treated according to his deserts, whereas few read the lives of famous criminals without some admiration of their daring and ingenuity; and we

I.]   COMPARISON WITH NAPOLEON I.   67

are affected by the same sentiments when we read of political crime, provided it is upon a grand enough scale.

Louis Napoleon resembles his great prototype up to a certain point. From his own lips we have a practical confession that in his life he was influenced by low ideas. While in exile he deliberately declared that he would rather be evil spoken of than not named at all. Up to this point then we see the resemblance, but the character of Louis Napoleon, in spite of his pertinacity, energy and sagacity, displayed neither consistency in virtue nor consistency in vice; either or both of which qualities would have enabled him to realise with more completeness the greater part of his magnificent conceptions. Doubtless if he had been a better man we should remember him with feelings very different from those with which we now turn away from the chequered spectacle of so much glory tarnished with so much shame. He commenced his public career by sullying his integrity, violating the most sacred obligations of gratitude, persecuting the innocent, tampering with justice, and expending upon intrigue an intellect obviously fitted for better things.

But to discuss whether or not his *coup d'état* merits an exception from that unqualified censure which is generally pronounced upon such actions, is to spin for ever on the same wheel round the same pivot. Controversies on speculative points of political philosophy always come round to the same insoluble problem as to whether ends justify means; but however evil the character of the *coup d'état* was considered at the time, Louis Napoleon might have lived down the disgrace of it in his subsequent career. There is scarcely any deed so black that it may not be obliterated by a man of great abilities; if those abilities are united with caution and patience, by a man who is a dangerous and yet a placable foe. We condone great faults in Napoleon I., because his deeds were so magnificent, because the man himself was so great that he seemed to tower above the conventional rules set forth for mankind. We condemn the faults of Louis Napoleon because he was possessed of no such greatness; because his measure of success fails to counterbalance the crimes which formed the inevitable complement of his exaltation. In the eyes of Europe he never lived down the falseness of his position. The great European Powers stigmatised him as an upstart, and his relations with other sovereigns were the same as those of a man of low extraction, who, on the strength of extraordinary success in trade, endeavours to make himself at home in an aristocratic society, with whom he never can really be assimilated, and from whom he continually receives reminders of his inferiority in social rank.

We are sometimes led to wonder under what conceivable circumstances the plans of Louis Napoleon could have succeeded. It must be remembered that he was not always the sport of European Powers. There was a time when sovereigns and statesmen trembled with fear lest he should succeed in establishing another empire after the pattern of the first. This dread, of course, only lasted so long as Europe over-rated his ability. It passed away when Louis Napoleon appeared in his true colours, and when he had thus shown himself to the world, men realised that he was not great enough to carry out the plans he had formulated. To this conclusion we must come, that even if fortune had not played him false, he never could have established his dynasty firmly on the throne. Bismarck said of him that people exaggerated his intellect, and this was doubtless the case. The only conceivable circumstances under which he might have succeeded, would have been if his reign had ended in the year 1863. Until that time, people had no opportunity for discovering the shiftiness and incoherence of his designs, his want of grasp on reality, and his absolute personal nullity as an administrator. Those who had formed any other conceptions of his character received a rude shock after that year. The repulse of his intervention on behalf of Poland, his inaction during the Danish War, showed those to be mistaken who sought in him a character like that of the great Napoleon. During the events which formed the first stage of the consolidation of Germany, his policy was one succession of errors, and the Mexican fiasco, besides weakening his resources at a time when concentrated strength alone could tell on European affairs, dissipated all the hopes and confidence that his admirers had placed in him. It was the over-estimating of his character by the French people that indirectly caused his ruin. When he first appeared upon the scene, his speech and his silence were invested with an equally awful significance. Such an assumption can only be verified by the accomplishment of great deeds, for the mere prestige of moral ascendancy is soon brought to the test of material success.

Louis Napoleon was called upon to exercise by moral ascendancy, which his character did not warrant him to possess, that sway over European councils which Napoleon I. failed to establish with arms. The wonder is that he succeeded as long as he did. The world looked for some substantial result of all this profound statecraft, and saw instead the pitiable spectacle of a vacillating monarch foiled by Cavour's cunning, by Bismarck's steadier resolve, and by the Pope's passive obstinacy. His infirmity of purpose, which seemed so out of keeping with the character he professed, enraged his subjects. It was said of him that he seemed everywhere to arrive one day too late, only to make up his mind when he had missed his opportunity. It is difficult, however, with all our speculation, to arrive at a true estimate of his character. His whole life is an enigma. There is nothing so remarkable as the absolute silence he observed towards those whose false advice had contributed to his ultimate humiliation. He would never contradict those who questioned his integrity, and even at the last he refused to take the world into the secret of his regrets and his remorse. In this, and in this alone, he contrasts favourably with the great Napoleon.

Lord Bacon once wrote that, "prosperity doth best discover vice, but adversity doth best discover virtue." Let us try to think this is true of Louis Napoleon. We cannot altogether despise him; we are rather compelled to regard him with mingled contempt and admiration; with mingled aversion and sympathy. We can come to one definite conclusion, that his life and his character were not of such kind to entitle him to that place in the world's history which from his boyhood he looked upon as his natural inheritance. His was a melancholy fate, and yet not undeserved. The best explanation of his career is offered in the words of Jules Lemaitre: "He had confusedly ruminated on the enfranchisement of nations, and the establishment of a Socialist and yet a Cæsarian democracy. These great designs were vaguely conceived by his imagination, the imagination of a gentle fatalist, who, dazzled by the prodigious destiny, of which he was the plaything, while believing himself to be its hero, had indolently confided in the virtue of his own star." The chief object in his life seems to have been to make himself great by whatever means, and without any very genuine consideration for the welfare of mankind. As the world progresses there is less and less room for such men. If they cannot show some more laudable objective, the world will cease to tolerate them.

Possessed of unquestionable ability of a kind, and some unusual gifts, Louis Napoleon owed much to fortune, and fortune for a time caressed him; but he came to count with too great a confidence on her favours, and in the hour of need he realised too late, that his confidence had been misplaced. It had been his aim to persuade his subjects that he was something more than mortal and when his conspicuous failures proved to the French people his mortality, they resented the deception which he had practised upon them, and they trampled their idol in the dust. Arriving then at these conclusions, we are bound to attach some significance to the cruel words of Victor Hugo: "Dieu l' a executé en le dégradant; Napoleon III. comme Empereur avait droit au tonnerre mais pour lui la tonnerre a été infamant, il a été foudroyé par derrière."

PART II
CAVOUR

"THE Italians need regeneration; their *morale* which was completely corrupted under the ignoble dominion of Spaniards and Austrians, regained a little energy under the French *régime*, and the ardent youth of the country sighs for a nationality; but to break entirely with the past, to be born anew to a better state, great efforts are necessary and sacrifices of all kinds must remould the Italian character. An Italian war would be a sure pledge that we were going to become again a nation, that we were rising from the mud in which we have been trampled for so many centuries." These pregnant sentences, written by Cavour when only in his twenty-second year, indicate the whole course of his subsequent endeavour to convert Italy from a mere geographical expression into a united kingdom. The policy which was to raise Sardinia from insignificance to elevate her to the level of Western Europe, to destroy the influence of Austria, to obtain at least one more province for Italy, to make sovereigns fly before popular demonstrations, and armies to dissolve before a band of adventurers, had its origin in Cavour. Whether the achievement of his life-work shall be for good or ill, time can alone show, but if internal prosperity and a rapidly increasing prestige among the nations of the world can be regarded as a test, Cavour's labours will not prove fruitless. At the very lowest estimation it must be claimed for Italy that she represents the triumph of the doctrine of nationalities in its best form. Nowhere else, it has been said, do so many elements of nationality concur; language, religion, a clearly defined geographical unity, a common literature and common sentiments, and with these advantages the Italians are undoubtedly beginning to realise the benefits to be derived from unity.

Italy owes her happier state to Mazzini, Victor Emmanuel, Garibaldi, and above all to Cavour, for he alone could reform administrations, assimilate states, evolve order from chaos, found legislative assemblies, and all the time prepare the way for future operations more hazardous and yet more effective and beneficial for his countrymen. Cavour, like Bismarck, knew how to tame the fierce spirit of revolution, to control it, and convert it to his own purposes. He knew how to shape the purposeless and meaningless demands of a people rendered frantic with the fever of revolution into definite and plausible aspirations. The Italians have not been slow to recognise the merit of their benefactors. The traveller in Italy at every turn is confronted by statues, more colossal perhaps than artistic, erected to the Four whose lives were spent in rendering the greatest service to their native land. There are yet some who deny that the Italians have been regenerated or that the country has derived any benefit from centralisation. Pessimists shake their heads and say that the political movements and combinations that make most noise in the world and excite the largest measure of enthusiasm are often not those which affect most deeply and most beneficially the real happiness of men, but those who will remember the insignificance of the country and the degradation of its people under the old *régime* will not deny to Cavour the fullest measure of praise. "Italia ab exteris liberanda" was the motto adopted by the apostles of the new political creed, and it was Cavour who inflamed the torpid minds of his fellow-countrymen with patriotic zeal. With the one great idea influencing his every thought and every action he achieved by his genius and enterprise a work, which on the evidence of history, was at once most difficult

HIS DEVOTION TO THE ITALIAN CAUSE

and most noble. In a small city on a rural stream surrounded by mountain peaks Cavour parleyed with every sovereign of Europe, and compromised himself with none, while he struggled on behalf of the greatest cause that it has ever fallen to the lot of a statesman to foster. It was no light task to uphold the prestige of an insignificant province among the councils of nations and to sustain the patriotism of his countrymen, but through it all he held in a firm grasp those famous Italian Republics that were never united except to face European armies in the field of battle.

The most singular combination of qualities, and the determination to devote all his energies to the cause, could alone achieve this herculean task. Amidst preoccupations of all sorts there was one ruling sentiment, a deep heartfelt conviction that never left him. Whether awake or dreaming, whether in the exultation of success or the despondency of failure, the thought of a united Italy raising her head amongst the great nations of the world cast into the shade every other thought, every other ambition. True it is that we find in history statesmen, and diplomatists, and scholars and heroes, but we find few instances of one like Cavour who could be all and more. The extent of his services must be measured by the whole interval between the year 1848 and the year 1861, an interval which although short enough in duration is charged with events that will fill a large volume in the history of the world, and the results of which have not yet been fully realised.

The regeneration of Italy, more than any other political movement has added popularity to the doctrine of the rights of nationalities. I would fain quote the words of Mr Lecky, no great lover of Italian unity, that give expression to the enthusiasm which it inspired:—

"Though some provinces sacrificed much, there was no province in which the Italian cause did not command the support of overwhelming majorities, and though two great wars and an overwhelming debt were the cost, the unity of Italy was at last achieved. The mingled associations of a glorious past and of a noble present, the genuine and disinterested enthusiasm that so visibly pervaded the great mass of the Italian people, the genius of Cavour, the romantic character and career of Garibaldi, and the inexpressible charm and loveliness of the land which was now rising into the dignity of nationhood, all contributed to make the Italian movement unlike any other of our time. It was the one moment of nineteenth century history when politics assumed something of the character of poetry."

Of Cavour's origin and early years it is necessary to record but little. He was born at Turin on the 10th of August in the year 1810. Through his father he was related to the old Piedmontese nobility, so that he inherited many of the privileges that good birth and high social rank can confer. As a child he hated his lessons, and was subject to violent fits of temper, but, despite these juvenile failings, as time advanced he exhibited some certain proof of the intelligence and judgment which in after years were to stand him in such good stead. At the age of ten he was sent to the Military Academy at Turin.

It was at this time that he received an appointment as page to the Prince of Carignan, heir-presumptive to the throne; but although the honour was bestowed upon him in recognition of his noble birth, he was so openly contemptuous of the dignity that he incurred disapproval in Court circles. Heedless of the consequences he consoled himself with study, and developed a *penchant* for mathematics that he declared was of great service to him in forming the habit of precise thought. It must be admitted that this branch of study is generally considered somewhat narrowing for the mind, and yet Cavour cultivated a vivid imagination, his sympathies were broad, and his training was anything but narrow. In fact few have enjoyed such varied experiences in early life, or have laid foundations of a political education, so deeply as Cavour. When he entered the army with the rank of lieutenant in the corps of Engineers, his liberal opinions became at once a hindrance to his ever taking kindly to the army as a profession. He saw in the idleness and apathy of the life in the solitary Alpine fortress of Bard, whither he had been sent on account of the language he had used in speaking of the July Revolution, a type of the disease from which the whole State was suffering. He detested this vegetable existence, and sought consolation in the works of Adam Smith, and in reading the various journals which at that time brought news of the English Reform Bill. So it soon came about that Cavour resigned his commission, and, his father having made for him the purchase of a small independent property near his ancestral estate at Leri, he retired thither to lead the simplest life, in this respect resembling his great German contemporary. It was not long before he entered with that zeal and interest, afterwards so proverbial, into the various occupations which the simple life of a bailiff can afford.

At first we are told it was as much as he could do to distinguish a cabbage from a turnip, and agriculture seemed to hold out but little attraction for him. He felt a certain repugnance for work which, as he himself expressed it, began with the analysis of dunghills, and ended in the middle of cattle-sheds; but he soon experienced a growing interest in his estate, and that which at first repelled him had now for him a charm which he never could have dreamed possible. He rose with the dawn, visited his cattle-sheds, was present at the departure of his labourers, superintended them perhaps under a burning sun, not satisfied with giving general directions, but looking to the minutest details, discerning the result with an almost infallible good sense, abandoning some experiments and repeating others on an immense scale with great attendant risk, and through all smiling, gay, and affable. In truth, however, he cared for politics before everything. Imbued with the spirit of the age, he became "absorbed in revolutions," and consequently, like others who have struck out a line of their own, he incurred the contemptuous surprise of his own family. At this period of his life, however, he knew in his heart that there was no chance to make a name for himself in the political world.

"If I were an Englishman," he sighs, "by this time I should be something, and my name would not be wholly unknown." The opportunity was lacking, but the ambition was ever present, and that, after all, is half the battle won. In his country retreat he watched the great movements of the world outside with an ever-increasing interest, and the fire of his energy was kept alive by an enthusiastic but hysterical lady who, steeped in the ideas of Mazzini, had enthralled the young Italian with her patriotic effusions and stirring appeals to his sentiment. Hysterical ladies, however, are sometimes dangerous, and it is perhaps well that Cavour escaped unharmed from this the only recorded love-entanglement of his life. Italy, he declared, was his "Sposa," and that he would never have another, although it was not for some time yet that he could claim his bride.

For fifteen years Cavour devoted his brain and his time to agricultural pursuits. Nowhere did he feel himself so thoroughly at home as at Leri. So attached did he become to the place that whenever during his subsequent career he wished to forget the cares of state it was there that he returned to refresh his mind and body. It must not be supposed that while in this retirement his energies were being wasted. The study of an estate can serve better purposes than the mere acquirement of agricultural skill, and Cavour gained a very considerable acquaintance with the social problems that lay at the root of the distressed condition of Italy. Moreover, he relieved the monotony of his retirement by visits to France and England, where he studied the working of those institutions which he desired to see introduced at home. The experience that he acquired during these rambles confirmed him in his opinion that society everywhere for good or for ill seemed to be making rapid strides towards democracy. Now it was in England that Cavour formed those friendships to which he so often referred afterwards with pride, and strengthened if he did not contract those habits of thought which, surviving the reproach of Anglomania have made his statesmanship a unique phenomenon in marked contrast with the peculiarities of Italian intellect and character. Unconsciously, then, at this period of his life Cavour was laying a solid foundation upon which he could, when the opportunity came, accomplish the great work of his life. Resembling many another great man in history he set out in life with one ruling idea, but with very little prospect of ever realising his ambitions, and without the remotest conception of how to carry out the scheme, but the idea being all-ruling, all-pervading, he had none of the temptations to enlarge his circle of interests which might have hindered the path to success; nor did he try to seek fortunes which, although they might lead him in the track of fame, would have enticed him away from the true object of his high endeavours. In only one direction did he wish to go, however insurmountable the obstacles, however distant the end might seem. "Happy or unhappy, my country shall have all my life; I will never be unfaithful to her, even were I sure of finding elsewhere a brilliant destiny."

Cavour's foremost ambition, conceived early in life, was to make Piedmont an object lesson in constitutional monarchy, and then to drive the Austrians out of Italy. These ends attained, he would leave it to the country whether it should decide to unite or not.

The career which was to fit him for this great work was soon to begin. On one of his visits to England, at a dinner of the Royal Geographical Society, Cavour delivered his maiden speech, which Lord Ripon, who happened to be present, declared was the augury of a successful public career. With awakening interest and with ever-increasing ardour he set himself to study the English agricultural system, the working of the new Poor Law, and the management of the English factories, hospitals, and prisons. He found time also to read with keen appreciation the lives of English statesmen; in fact he had now become thoroughly imbued with English ideas and the liberal tendencies of modern Europe.

On his return to Italy he discovered that, after eight months of Paris and London, to fall back abruptly on Turin, without transition, from the *salons* of the Duc de Broglie, and the Marquis of Lansdowne into those where the retrograde spirit reigned unopposed, the fall was violent. Yet he believed that under the present political conditions in Italy he could best serve his country by keeping himself in reserve, for, like a true patriot, he thought that small concessions were useless, perhaps more worthless than no concessions at all.

In 1847, however, he awoke to the fact that the press had suddenly become an important influence in the political world, so he left his farm to found, in conjunction with Count Cesare Balbo, a newspaper, to which was given the ominous title, *Il Risorgimento*. The aims and objects of this journal were said to be independence, union between princes and people, and finally reforms. The tone of the political articles which he contributed to this paper may not be palatable to modern taste, but Cavour had to engage very different readers from those who seek intellectual enjoyment merely. In the words of M. de la Rive, " he had not to amuse but to instruct; to enlighten a public hitherto kept in ignorance, desirous of knowing, anxious to comprehend, sincere, serious." This ungrateful task he fulfilled with the capacity and the conscience of a man who seemed specially prepared for it by the solidity and the diversity of his knowledge.

Cavour, now thoroughly convinced that a constitutional monarchy was the only form of government in Italy which could combine freedom with order, made no delay in petitioning for what he wanted through the medium of the press, at the same time laying all his plans with caution and with studious regard for the welfare of his countrymen. It was due in a large measure to these methods of preparing the people gradually for liberty that a reign of terror like that in France did not replace a reign of corruption. He wished for the present to be cautious, and he was resolved not to purchase freedom for Italy at the price of general confusion, political and social. "I desire this crisis with all the precautions conformable to the state of things, and I am, moreover, thoroughly persuaded that the premature attempts of the men of the movement do but retard this crisis and make it more hazardous." Cavour wrote with the practical object of thus training the popular mind, and he took great pains to organise a moderate liberal party for this purpose, capable at need of restraining the ultras; but he found himself excluded from office in the momentous year of revolutions.

II.] THE POLICY OF BOLD COUNSELS IN 1848

The new Cabinet entered upon their duties in March 1848, and hardly had the Ministers met when they received news of an event totally unforeseen—the rising of Milan against the Austrians. In a few days the intelligence reached Turin and drew forth instantly a passionate outburst from the pen of Cavour in the columns of the *Risorgimento,* pointing out that only one course lay open for the hesitating king, and that was war. "In our position," he wrote, "there is but one policy—not the policy of the Louis Philippes and Guizots, but the policy of the Fredericks the Great, the Napoleons and the Charles Emmanuels; the great policy—the policy of bold counsels." Bold the counsels certainly were, nor were they disregarded, for on the same evening as the article was published the king made up his mind, and war was declared on the 25th day of the month. Into the details of the subsequent hostilities it is not within the scope of this work to enter. Suffice it to say, that after the fatal battle of Novara the king was forced to abdicate in favour of his son.

It must be borne in mind that Cavour, even in the year 1848, was never an advocate of what he was pleased to call revolutionary means; those same revolutionary means that led to Waterloo and St Helena, that produced the siege of Paris, that placed Louis Napoleon on the throne, and that had wrecked the fairest and justest revolutions. His main object had been during the unfortunate year of 1848, and the first months of 1849, to stem the war current and to keep watch over the Constitution, which each of the extreme parties, the reactionary and the revolutionary was equally anxious to sweep away. He had a difficult task before him, and a man of less moral courage would have broken down under the weight of abuse and calumny which he provoked and confronted. He strenuously opposed the ultra democrats, and during this disastrous period of alternate hopes and fears, spasmodic efforts and half-hearted co-operation, he had remained in the background, but the fatal campaign that ended with Novara marked the turning point in his career. He was re-elected when Victor Emmanuel dissolved his first Parliament by what is known as the proclamation of Moncalieri; and in the debates on the Foro Ecclesiastico for the first time he made his power felt in the Chamber.

He was destined now to emerge one of the foremost figures in Italy, taking an intermediate place between the moderates and the party of action, thus reconciling the practical aims of the one with the comprehensive patriotism of the

other, but he joined the Ministry not without
grave misgivings, because he thought that his
part would soon be played out. "I am half
used up already" he said at the time, "I shall
be so wholly before long." Nevertheless he still
cherished a hope that the priesthood would
recognise the necessity to modern society of the
two great moral forces, religion and liberty; and
when once this conversion had been accomplished
the pathway to large and fearless reforms would
be open. From 1849 onward, Cavour's career
naturally divides itself into four periods.

The earliest represents his home policy, first
as the colleague of Massimo d'Azeglio, and
afterwards as President of the Council up to
the commencement of hostilities in the Crimea.
The second includes the Crimean War and its
immediate consequences to Sardinia. The third
extends from 1856 to the cession of Nice and
Savoy. The last and greatest, only his premature
death interrupted. Cavour entered the political
arena with all eyes turned upon him as the one
Italian who was strong enough for the task of
freeing Italy from the yoke of the foreigner, and
it was not long before the hopes of his fellow-
countrymen were to be realised. As Minister of
Commerce he negotiated treaties with France,
England and Belgium, and, on the strength of

his success he was appointed Minister of Marine. In these two capacities he gradually assumed the leadership of the House. Taking upon himself also the management of the Finance Department he felt at last well equipped to turn his attention with some effect to the realisation of his ambitions.

At first, however, aid must be evoked from outside. With the assistance of the French Government it might be possible to shake off the Austrian yoke, but any alliance with France seemed to him a remote and doubtful contingency, so that, while he always held it in view, he did not forget that before all things Piedmont must be consolidated as a constitutional state. If that were not done a new Bonaparte might, indeed, cross the Alps in the character of liberator, but a free Italy would be no more the result of his intervention than it had been under the auspices of the great Emperor.

To comprehend Cavour's next move it is necessary here to explain briefly the state of parties in the Sardinian Chamber of Deputies. This was composed of the Right Centre, Liberal Conservatives; the Extreme Right, loyal to the House of Savoy, but opposed to Italian aspirations; the Left Centre, moderate Liberals and the Extreme Left, strongly Italian with its motto, "Long live Victor, the Provisional King." Now the two centres seemed irreconcilable, for, after the *coup d'état* the Extreme Right professed to believe that a free state wedged in between the despotisms of France and Austria was impossible. To crush this party Cavour formed a junction with Rattazzi, the brilliant leader of the Left Centre. This political manœuvre was somewhat unconstitutionally kept a secret, but Cavour, acting, as he was, upon public grounds, satisfied his conscience that the "Connubio," as it was derisively called, should be an accomplished fact before it was exposed by discussion. Unconstitutional such a proceeding may have been, but let us remember that such tactics have been frequently used and found efficient by more modern if less moral statesmen. D'Azeglio strongly disapproved of Rattazzi, and so it became necessary for Cavour to place his resignation in the hands of the King, who informed his late Minister that it might be some time before he was recalled to power.

Cavour accordingly left Italy for a visit to France and to England. In London he was warmly welcomed by Lord Malmesbury, the English Foreign Minister, and he received the assurance that the English Government would be glad to see him back in office. Lord Palmerston went a step further, and promised the moral support, not of one party or another, but of England. Enchanted with his reception he left for Paris, where he met with such encouragement from Louis Napoleon and from his Minister that he then and there wrote the significant words: "Whether we like it or not our destinies depend on France; we must be her partner in the great game which will be played sooner or later in Europe." On his return from this successful mission he found the Ministry in trouble, having rejected a Bill for permitting civil marriage, which in the opinion of the Pope seemed a euphemism for concubinage.

The King, on the consequent resignation of d'Azeglio, sent for Cavour, but would only allow him to form a Ministry on the condition that he would make up the quarrel with Rome. This Cavour flatly refused to do, with the gratifying result that Victor Emmanuel, convinced at last that he was the only statesman for the crisis, charged him to form a Ministry without any stipulations.

On entering upon office he immediately set himself the task of regenerating Piedmont, which had been left destitute of all the necessary accessories of modern life; by completing the railway system, by extending the roads and canals, and by encouraging all branches of industry. "It must not be forgotten," he explained, "that we have adopted a policy of action—a policy of progress. In order to re-establish the equilibrium of our finances we have deliberately resolved not to restrict our expenditure and by so doing renounce every idea of improvement and every great enterprise; not to endeavour by every species of economy to bring our expenditure within our income, but rather to effect our end by promoting all works of public utility, by developing the elements of progress which our State possesses, and by stimulating in every portion of our country all the industrial and economical activity of which it is found capable."

But improvement of any sort is usually expensive, and in this instance Cavour was obliged to increase the taxation by fourteen million francs. The lower classes of most nations like to see improvements and progress, but they are always more willing to live on obstinately in their old state than to draw from their pockets the money requisite for those sound reforms, which in the long run will repay them a thousandfold. The popularity of the Minister was not therefore enhanced. In October 1853 Cavour's house was attacked, and he himself was threatened, but the great patriot was wise in his generation. He alone was provident enough to realise that Piedmont needed a long period of active and consecutive labour before it could enter the lists again as armed champion of Italian independence, and it was with this object in view that he set to work industriously to strengthen the resources of his native country. Long ere this he had published his ideas on reform: "The railroads will stretch without interruption from the Alps to Sicily, and will cause to disappear all the obstacles and distances which separate the inhabitants of Italy, and hinder them from forming a great and single nation."

While Cavour was thus engaged, certain enigmatical remarks, uttered by Louis Napoleon, reached his ears, and these vague reports decided the bold policy that he subsequently adopted. In January 1854 he sounded the King as to whether he thought that his government might extract some advantage from the war of the Western Powers with Russia. The King seemed to reply in the affirmative, but the body of the people was against Cavour, and denounced the project in a summary manner as economically reckless, militarily a folly, and politically a crime. Cavour stood undeterred by these severe comments. His prospects of success did not seem to him so gloomy as might have been expected under the circumstances. An alliance with Piedmont was a popular notion in England, and Austria, after some delay, had signed a treaty which appeared to prevent her from taking sides with Russia; a situation that seemed decidedly to favour his policy.

On the 10th of January in the following year Cavour took over the Foreign Office, and on the same day the protocol of the offensive and defensive alliance of Sardinia with France and England was at last signed. Cavour had by this time come to the conclusion that plots and revolutions could not make the Italian kingdom. The raising of her credit seemed the only remedy for the deplorable condition into which the country had sunk. To raise Italy's credit two things were needed; the proof that an Italian Government could combine order with liberty, and the proof that Italians could fight.

Since it had pleased Providence that Piedmont alone in Italy should be free and independent, Piedmont was bound to make use of this freedom and independence to plead before Europe the cause of the unhappy peninsula. This perilous task the King and the country were resolved to persevere in to the end. What Cavour most feared was, not so much defeat as inaction and reaction, the moral effect of which he knew would be the greatest obstacle to his ambitions. On 16th August the Piedmontese were able to rejoice over a small victory won on the Tchernaia, and they read with pride the accounts of the sufferings so bravely borne by their little army. No less than twelve hundred died of cholera, but their courage and fortitude had served to convert the public to Cavour's war policy.

Cavour has incurred the gravest charges for the part he took in the Crimean War, through the medium of various writers and speakers; but it must be borne in mind that his object in sending Sardinian troops to the front was not so much on account of hostile intent against Russia as that he might find allies in England and France to help him in the work of uniting Italy. He believed, too, that the Italians in the Crimean War would gain glory, political consideration, the esteem of other Powers, and moral preponderance; whereas if they had been left out of the European combination, Piedmont would have fallen back into insignificance, and Italy would remain a geographical expression. Those who accuse him of making use of immoral means to attain his ends must take into consideration that he undoubtedly had a stronger motive for going to war, and achieved more effectual results from that war than any other Power concerned.

At this time Victor Emmanuel and Cavour visited England. Queen Victoria expressed so much sympathy with the aims of the latter, that he called her "the best friend of Piedmont in England," but in this hour of triumph rumours of peace came as a violent shock to Victor Emmanuel, who had hoped that the war would last long enough for Russia to be placed in real danger, with the result that Austria would be obliged then to go to her assistance. Meanwhile, in Piedmont itself, a well-sustained quarrel continued between Church and State which threatened Cavour's position. The question of the abolition of religious corporations had been again taken into consideration, and Cavour had made several overtures to the Vatican for a settlement without any result. In a temperate speech he pointed out that it was only needful to compare the countries where the monks and friars abounded in number and influence to determine whether it was possible to allege that they tended to enlightenment and prosperity. The Bill was passed in the Chamber of Deputies in March 1855, and the King was soon after approached by the Archbishop of Novara, who promised to make up the sum which the Government expected to gain by the suppressions if the Bill were withdrawn. The Chamber refused, and accordingly Cavour and his Ministry were obliged to resign. Personally, the King had always a certain sense of relief in parting with Cavour, and fondly imagined that he could get along very well without his aid.

The country, however, was by this time in a state of chronic agitation, and the present crisis required a strong hand at the helm, if the storm was to be safely weathered. There seemed no satisfactory substitute for Cavour forthcoming, and d'Azeglio did wisely in counselling the King to recall the fallen Minister. The advice was acted upon, and an amended form of the Bill, which had been the source of trouble, passed through the Chamber. Meanwhile the eyes of the people were turned away from domestic concerns to become fixed upon the conflict in the East, and to realise its significance to Italy.

Now it so happened, that in the year 1856, neither the French nor the English Government, was in a mood that promised anything to Italian aspirations. Cavour then did not believe that any good would come of the Congress of Paris. However, he asked Massimo d'Azeglio to represent Sardinia there, but the latter would only fulfil this duty on the condition that he should be

II.]   THE CONGRESS OF PARIS IN 1856   99

received on an equality with the representatives of the greater Powers. Cavour tried in vain to conceal from him the fact that France and England were determined that Sardinia should have a voice only in Sardinian affairs. On discovering the truth d'Azeglio refused to go, and there was no alternative but that Cavour should take his place. In January he had sent a memorandum, short and moderate in tone, which, indicating the course that Louis Napoleon should adopt in the interests of Italy, recommended the evacuation of Bologna by the Austrians. He set out then for Paris, needlessly doubting his powers of diplomacy, and wondering how it was possible to plead the cause of Italy in a congress where Austria had a voice. A few days after his arrival he was informed that the Emperor, in concert with England, conceded the point as to placing the representative of Sardinia on the same footing with those of the greater Powers. Encouraged by this concession, Cavour set to work to enlist in his service all those who might be willing to help the cause he had at heart, even going so far as to make a convert of a fair Countess, to whose charms Louis Napoleon is supposed to have fallen a victim, while his chief instrument was a certain Dr Conneau, who became henceforth the intermediary between himself and the Emperor.

Now at the earlier sittings of the Congress, Cavour kept in the background, as he felt obliged to proceed in the business he had undertaken with a degree of caution and restraint which few men would have had the self-control to observe. A short while before the signature of peace he brought before the notice of the English and French plenipotentiaries the Austrian occupation of the Roman legations. At a supplementary sitting on the 8th of April, after the signing of peace, Count Walewski, at the instance of Louis Napoleon, proposed to a bewildered audience, a discussion on the French and Austrian occupations of the Roman States, and the conduct of the King of Naples, as likely to provoke grave complications, and to compromise the peace of Europe. Cavour then had at last triumphed. Not the least of his achievements at the Congress was his private conversation with Lord Clarendon. The English Minister, worked up to indignation, burst forth in a fit of passion against the French occupation in Rome, and the Austrian occupation at Bologna.

Cavour had explained to Lord Clarendon that there were two results of the Congress which could affect Italy: firstly, that Austria was determined to make no concession; and secondly, that Italy had nothing to expect from diplomacy. For Sardinia, there were two alternatives; either

A MORAL VICTORY

she must be reconciled to the Pope, and to Austria, or there must be war, and in that case it would be war to the knife. Lord Clarendon readily concurred with these opinions, and although in subsequent years he publicly denied ever having encouraged Piedmont to go to war with Austria, he doubtless let fall some sentences which gave Cavour to understand that England would proffer her assistance when required. Fortified with such a hope, Cavour, shortly after the Congress, paid a visit to England to make sure of the ground upon which he was treading. It was a wise move indeed, for no sooner had he arrived there than he discovered that neither Lord Clarendon nor Lord Palmerston seemed very enthusiastic on his behalf. Nevertheless, he returned to Italy congratulating himself on a moral victory, although he had gained no material advantage for the present. His Tuscan compatriots, moreover, caused him further elation by sending him a bust of himself with an inscription from Dante, which ran:

"He who defended her with open face."

If then he had achieved no other result, he had at any rate roused the minds of his countrymen, and protest in Piedmont gave way to defiance. But circumstances still seemed to combine to isolate Cavour, and yet the more isolated he became the less he seemed to fear.

Louis Napoleon was hesitating, according to his wont, Austria was detaching herself from Russia, and drawing closer to England, and Palmerston now suspected Cavour of being too friendly with Russia. But Cavour remained bold, energetic, and determined in the face of all difficulties. In August 1856, the first interview between himself and Garibaldi took place, an interview that was to produce such far-reaching consequences. At this time he also engaged in a secret intercourse with Giuseppe La Farina, a Sicilian exile, who had chosen for his watchword, "Italy under Victor Emmanuel." His meetings with Farina took place in the early morning before it grew light, for fear that Parliament or Diplomacy should get wind of these secret negotiations. With cunning sagacity and courage he was laying his plans for the great movement that was to make Italy once again a united whole, and that was to free his countrymen from the yoke of the foreigner.

Cavour now took over the management of the Foreign Office with the approval of the people, who were at length thoroughly convinced that he alone could deliver their country from its deplorable predicament. One of his first acts after the Congress of Paris was to force Parliament to vote the supplies required for undertaking the boring of the Mont Cenis Tunnel, an enterprise which drew forth from Lord Palmerston the famous comment, " Henceforth no one will talk of the work of the ancient Romans." His next move was to consign the Exchequer to Lauza ; assuming himself the Ministry of the Interior. So far all seemed well, but an unfortunate episode occurred at this time which endangered the friendly relations existing between himself and the King. Cavour had wished to put an end to the King's relations with the Countess Mirafiori, with results which such interference only can entail, and just as everything was working ill for Cavour's cause, to make matters worse, the Archduke Maximilian had come to Milan to kill Italian opposition to Austria with his kindness. But Cavour was not to be done out of his *casus belli*. Although he feared that the Italians would be won over by Maximilian, an incident occurred in the beginning of the year 1858 which eventually turned out completely in his favour. This was the attempt of Felice Orsini to assassinate Louis Napoleon. At first Cavour was in the utmost dismay. Conscious that single handed the risk of attacking the Austrian power was greater than he could wisely undertake, he believed that he had found a firm supporter in the French Emperor, but now the attempt of Orsini threatened for the instant to break down even this support. It was generally suspected that the Republican refugee had attempted to take the Emperor's life in revenge for his supposed opposition to the free development of Italy.

Louis Napoleon, affecting to be enraged with the Sardinian Government, caused a very sharp despatch to be sent to Sardinia demanding a change in the law for the protection of foreign rulers. The misunderstanding, which might easily have interrupted the friendship of France and Sardinia, was removed by a straightforward autograph letter from Victor Emmanuel, which Cavour instructed General Della Rocca, who had been sent to congratulate the Emperor on his escape, to "commit the indiscretion" of reading word by word. This plan produced the desired effect, and Louis Napoleon sent back a conciliatory message to Victor Emmanuel which seemed to end the whole affair, although Cavour still found it necessary to keep the Emperor's attention fixed on Italy by assuring him that if worst came to the worst Sardinia was ready to go to war with Austria by herself.

Louis Napoleon was rapidly coming round to

Cavour's views, and it is certain now that Orsini's attempt, abortive though it was, furthered the cause for which he died. Not only was the Emperor stirred to fresh endeavour on behalf of the Italian cause by the dying prayers of the assassin, but he was also powerfully influenced by a desire to withdraw the French garrison, which, in conjunction with the Austrians, was upholding the Pope against the change of government so ardently desired by the Roman people. Moreover, the advice which he thought himself justified under the circumstances in pressing upon the Pope was disregarded, and the influence of Austria seemed paramount. He was therefore weary of supporting a court where he was unable to make his voice fully heard, and so it happened that in the month of June, under the seal of secrecy, it was arranged by Dr Conneau that Louis Napoleon and Cavour should meet "by accident" at Plombières. The Italian Minister forthwith started for the venue, not without a grave misgiving that he would "commit some stupidity." At Plombières he passed nearly the whole of two days closeted with Louis Napoleon, the decisive interview lasting from 11 A.M. to 3 P.M., after which the Emperor took him out alone in a carriage driven by himself. Cavour came away with great hopes, but without absolute assurance. Like other European statesmen, he entertained a certain measure of distrust, not without cause, for the great adventurer.

In the meantime, however, some definite conclusions had been arrived at. The object of the war was to be the expulsion of the Austrians from the peninsula, to be followed by the formation of a kingdom of Upper Italy which should include the valley of the Po, the legations and the marches of Ancona; Savoy and Nice to be ceded to France. Finally, much against the wish of Victor Emmanuel, Cavour was determined to gratify Louis Napoleon by urging that historical nuptial outrage, the marriage of the king's daughter, Clotilde, to Prince Jerome Napoleon, the worst of his race, for "reasons of state." All that was defective in these international arrangements Cavour excused by the explanation that in politics it is only possible to do one thing at a time, and the only object that Italians had now to aim at was the expulsion of the Austrians from Italy. If in these negotiations Cavour erred, he erred in common with great and high-minded statesmen who, driven to elect between expediency of the highest order and duty vanishing into a sentiment, have given a casting vote to the former.

Cavour paid no heed to the gloomy forebodings of his colleagues and of foreign ambassadors.

He even told Lord Odo Russell in December of 1858 that he intended to force Austria to declare war, and at the same interview expressed his belief that the consummation of his desire would take place about the first week in May. But he still feared the risk of French influence extending over Italy, and to ward off such a danger he was determined that not only the Government and the army but Italian patriots of every condition, should rally round the flag. His first project then was to place in the field some thousands of volunteers in spite of the objections raised by generals in the army, and having secured the co-operation of Garibaldi, he carried out this plan without the assent of Parliament, and at the risk of offending Louis Napoleon, in dealing with whom he thought that the best course would be to show a bold front. Be it remembered, to their eternal credit, that the King and d'Azeglio, both of whom had very just cause to dislike him, extended their whole-hearted support to his cause. Nor was their confidence misplaced. Cavour possessed the written agreement of Plombières, and threatened if he were deserted to publish it, and thus ruin the Emperor's credit at home and abroad.

On the 1st of January in the year 1859 Louis Napoleon gave utterance to the ominous words in conversation with the Austrian Ambassador: "Je regrette que les relations entre nous soient si mauvaises." Thus far had Cavour already influenced the French Emperor, but his full powers of diplomacy were now to be revealed in an episode which bears a striking resemblance to the ruse which Bismarck resorted to when he despatched the famous Ems telegram.

Cavour, after having composed the speech from the throne, sent a draft to Louis Napoleon for correction. The French Emperor sent back an amended version which Cavour had translated into good Italian, omitting here a word or inserting here a phrase. The critical sentence in the Emperor's draft ran as follows: "While respecting treaties we cannot remain insensible to the cries of grief that reach us from so many parts of Italy."

On the 10th of January the King delivered the corrected version of the speech, with the telling result that Cavour had looked for, and not long afterwards Louis Napoleon authorised a treaty to be signed, binding France to come to the assistance of Piedmont, if that State were the object of an act of aggression on the part of Austria. In Parliament Cavour managed to obtain a vote for fifty million francs, and although Lord Derby had declared that Austria was only seeking to improve its Italian provinces, Cavour believed that in England there was much suppressed sympathy with his cause. Nor was he slow to recognise that it was necessary to conciliate England in order to obtain her help when it might be required in the future, as it doubtless would be, to drive the French out of Italy. All his hopes, however, seemed dashed to the ground when he perceived that Louis Napoleon, awaking to the fact that no one except the Paris workmen desired war, was looking for a retreat from his engagements with the Italian Minister in the Russian proposal of a congress. Hastening to Paris he interviewed the Emperor, but with no satisfactory result to himself. The English Government brought forward a proposal that all the Italian States should be admitted to the Congress, and that Austria, as well as Piedmont should be invited to disarm. Cavour felt bound to consent to the plan. In the utmost misery of despair he contemplated suicide, but the folly of Count Buol, the Austrian Minister, saved the situation for him in the nick of time. Count Buol had sent off a contemptuous reply to the English Government saying that Austria herself would call upon Piedmont to disarm, which truculent attitude left only one course open to the French Emperor.

When Cavour left the Chamber of Deputies after plenary powers had been conferred upon the King, he significantly remarked to a friend who brought him the news of the Austrian ultimatum, "I am leaving the last sitting of the last Piedmontese Chamber!"

The Austrian ultimatum consisted of the following chief demands. Firstly, that the Sardinian army should be placed on a peace footing, and secondly, that the volunteers should be dismissed. An answer was required within three days. Cavour's curt reply was to the effect that Piedmont had decided to accept proposals made by England with the approval of France, Prussia, and Russia. The French Ambassador at Vienna simultaneously instructed Count Buol that his sovereign would consider the crossing of the frontier by the Austrian troops equivalent to a declaration of war. Cavour on his part took leave of the Austrian Ambassador with studied courtesy, and then turning to those present delivered himself of the remarkable sentence: "We have made history; now let us go to dinner." So far all seemed well. To achieve his ends Cavour had recourse to means which must strictly be characterised as immoral. He was obliged to enter into communication with some of the revolutionary party who had hitherto been at enmity with all crowns alike. He had to convince Garibaldi in secret that he ought to take part in this war; Garibaldi, a man, who, as a defender of the Roman Republic, must have been obnoxious to Louis Napoleon. He had to conceal from Louis Napoleon the fact that Garibaldi would be at the head of a free corps at the side of the allied armies. He had to raise from the Savoyards their last farthing in taxation, and at the same time to drive them to the camp, only to surrender them after victory to a foreign power. He had to goad Austria to an act of passion, and finally he had to bargain away the daughter of his sovereign.

But, in considering these political transactions, it must be remembered that he would have deemed it the greatest crime to have left undone anything which might contribute to the great object of Italian unity. He bid a high price for success, and now it was within his grasp. He had not been done out of his allies, and he had not been done out of his *casus belli*. Nor, when hostilities commenced, did he seem unequal to the occasion. He proved an energetic and capable Minister of War. During the actual campaign he had a bed placed near to his office, and during the nights he walked in his dressing-gown from one department to another, giving directions as to police regulations and all details connected with the War Office. He was not tortured by misgivings, the thought which was uppermost in his mind was that the Sardinian army, which he had worked so hard to make efficient, was doing Italy credit. The war for Cavour meant triumph and repose. It consecrated his policy and quieted his mind.

The Austrian army, under their incompetent general, Ginlay, after crossing the Ticino, came to a full stop, and their delay was the occasion for a Piedmontese victory at Palestro. Ginlay found himself outflanked and compelled to retire. The allies followed him and defeated the Austrian army in its position about Magenta, on the road to Milan. The victory of the allies was at once felt throughout Central Italy, and everywhere the demand was for union with Piedmont. The Liberals in Tuscany, Parma, Modena and Romagna were preparing to chase away the petty despots who ruled under Austrian control, although Victor Emmanuel still avoided any negotiations with those States which might compromise him with Europe, contenting himself merely with appointing Commissioners to enrol troops for the common war against Austria, and to conduct the necessary work of adminstration in these districts.

As yet Lombardy had alone been won, but towards the end of June the allies came into contact once again with the Austrians about Solferino, and there was fought one of the bloodiest battles of modern times, ending with a victory for French arms. Cavour's dream now seemed within measurable distance of realisation, when suddenly in the first days of July he received the intelligence that Louis Napoleon had sought an interview with Francis Joseph at Villafranca. The results of this conference drove Cavour to such a pitch of frenzy that many were in apprehension for his life and reason. Lombardy was to be given up, but the Duchies were to be restored to their late rulers, and Venetia, still remaining a part of the Austrian Empire, was to become one of a confederation of Italian States under the presidency of the Pope.

The French Emperor thus seemed to have unravelled all that Cavour had taken so much pains to bind together, and to complete his misery, news arrived that six Prussian army corps were ready to move for the Rhine frontier. It must be owned that Cavour lost his head at this crisis. He rushed to Victor Emmanuel's headquarters to advise him either to refuse Lombardy and abdicate, or to continue the war by himself. The King was sitting calm and resigned, listening to a French officer reading the preliminaries of the Treaty in the presence of La Marmora when Cavour entered. The Minister, forgetting all self-respect, stormed at his master, upbraiding him with his complaisance, but the King on his side kept his temper, and quietly signed the preliminaries, "pour ce qui me concerne."

It was like some fearsome nightmare to Cavour to see all his darling projects scattered to the winds at one fell stroke. His first thought had been to go and be killed at Bologna, if, as was expected, there was to be fighting there; but in the midst of his frenzy there suddenly flashed upon him a determination that this Treaty should never be carried out. He returned soberly to Turin, and shortly afterwards resigned office, his last act being to despatch ten thousand muskets to Farina at Modena.

His resignation was not dictated, as might be supposed, either by anger or discouragement. He still had full faith in the triumph of the cause for which he had striven, and he was still ready to devote to it what of life might yet be spared to him, but he was convinced that at this particular moment his participation in public affairs would only be hurtful to his country. It suited his purpose to appear cool and calculating, while in reality he had only retreated that he might leap the better.

Whether Cavour's schemes were now to succeed or fail depended henceforth largely upon England. In that country the Liberals had just gained a majority, a circumstance of inestimable advantage to the Italian cause. The Liberal Ministry would have nothing to do with either French or Austrian aggression in Italy. Lord Palmerston declared that the French formula of " Italy given to herself" had been transferred into " Italy sold to Austria," while he firmly believed that Cavour's object was the good of Italy. Moreover, since the Italians refused with complete unanimity to receive back the rulers of the Duchies, and had quietly carried on provisional governments in the name of the Sardinian King, it was now sufficiently clear that the Western Powers would never consent to force being employed for the purpose of imposing upon the Italians any form of government or constitution. Austria accordingly yielded, and the Italian States, having declared their wishes by unmistakable majorities, were annexed to the Sardinian monarchy.

Meanwhile Cavour had been trying to upset the Ministry. Rattazzi, on his part, had calumniated Cavour in order to keep him out of office, but after the peace of Zurich the popular demand for the appointment of Cavour as Sardinian plenipotentiary was too strong to be resisted. Great moderation and good taste were now exhibited on the part of all persons concerned. The King agreed to forget the interview at Villafranca; Rattazzi, who could not have appreciated the idea of Cavour working with him, yielded to the necessities of the situation; and, finally, Cavour, who could not have appreciated the idea of serving under Rattazzi, accepted the post in order to prevent an antagonism which might have proved fatal to the cause of Italian unity. So all three men were compelled to make a virtue of necessity, and Cavour found himself back again in power on the high road to the premiership.

On Cavour's return to power M. Guizot is reported to have said: "Two men divide the attention of Europe at the present moment; the Emperor and M. de Cavour. The game has commenced, and I should bet on M. de Cavour." Long ere this Cavour had made up his mind that the only way out of all difficulties was to strike a direct bargain with Louis Napoleon, who now only held out in order to sell his consent. He was convinced that the cession of the two provinces was an act of necessity; provided that the will of the people of Savoy was first taken. He believed, as he said, that the true ground for the cession of Savoy and Nice, lay in the fact that the Treaty was an integral part of the Italian policy, the logical and inevitable consequences of a past policy, and an absolute necessity for the carrying out of this policy in the future. Accordingly, on 24th March, he signed the secret Treaty. Secret it was, although he had endeavoured to induce Louis Napoleon to let it be submitted to Parliament, according to constitutional usage, before any signature was attached.

It came about then that at the Parliament which met in April 1860, to efface the frontier lines of six states, the man who had done so much for the uniting of Italy now incurred the impeachment that he had dismembered his native land.

There was no lack of opponents, foul-mouthed slanderers, who were prepared at this crisis to ruin the career of the great patriot. It is a singular circumstance that distinguished statesmen of all countries and of all epochs in history, who have been possessed with a laudable desire to enhance the greatness and the welfare of their native land, have always been subject to the indignity of refuting groundless attacks on their personal integrity, emanating from impudent and envious nonentities whose insignificance is only surpassed by their inability to confine themselves to the truth. Cavour answered the attack with strength and dignity, but although the Treaty was sanctioned by a majority he never recovered from the taunts of his opponents, although he was yet destined to be re-established in the fulness of power and popularity.

Scarcely had the Treaty of Cession received Parliamentary ratification when Garibaldi set out for Genoa to effect the liberation of Sicily and Naples. Smarting under the separation of his birthplace Nice from the Italy for which he had so earnestly fought, and trusting to enthusiasm rather than to political combination, he secretly equipped at Genoa two steamers, and with a force of about a thousand volunteers embarked for Sicily.

It is difficult perhaps for us to decide how far Cavour was responsible for this move which ended in the annexation of Naples to the new kingdom. We only know that a formal disapproval of it appeared in the official gazette. Cavour had sought to re-establish relations of friendship with King Francis II., whose father Ferdinand had set the whole of Europe about his ears, by his friendship shown to Russia during the Crimean War, and by his tyrannical system of government at home. Cavour now renewed his demand that the King should enter into alliance with Piedmont, accepting a constitutional system of government, and the national Italian policy of Victor Emmanuel, but he failed to produce any real change in the spirit of the Neapolitan court.

After a further warning from Victor Emmanuel the revolutionary forces of Garibaldi were let loose against the stubborn Francis. Cavour did not attempt to hinder this move, only making a stipulation that Garibaldi's expedition should not molest Sardinia. For a whole week, during which time no news of the expedition arrived, gloomy forebodings possessed his mind, but on the evening of 13th May a passer-by in the Via Carlo Alberto heard some one gaily whistling an air. Of a sudden the individual, who was walking very swiftly, vigorously rubbed his hands. It was none other than Cavour. He had just received the intelligence that Garibaldi, eluding the Neapolitan fleet, had disembarked with all his men at Marsala. Although he himself had already at this time begun to contemplate the overthrow of the Bourbon dynasty at Naples, he yet saw the danger of compromising his Government with the great European Powers.

The English Government alone for the present applauded the Sicilian scheme. When, however, Palermo was successfully captured, Cavour recognised that the time had come for further steps towards Italian union, and he now wished that Sicily should be annexed at once, although he was apprehensive of the Garibaldian dictatorship, which he seriously believed might entail war with Austria. He accordingly wished that an end might be put to the resistance of Naples before Garibaldi assumed dictatorial power in Naples itself, and with this object he had recourse to those Machiavellian means which the greatest of statesmen have generally considered expedient, if not necessary, under similar circumstances. Working upon the principle that when one course becomes inevitable it is no good counting up its dangers, but rather to endeavour to overcome them, he cast hesitation aside when the news of Garibaldi's victory at Milazzo, and the evacuation of Messina reached Turin. He ordered Admiral Persano to leave two ships of war to cover Garibaldi's passage to the mainland, and with one ship to proceed to Naples himself, and there excite insurrection and win the Neapolitan fleet to the flag of Victor Emmanuel. The subsequent march of Garibaldi on the capital was one continuous triumph, but Cavour, now dreading the dictatorship of the great General more than before, tried by all means in his power to provoke the revolution and contrive the expulsion of King Francis, in order to establish a government of some kind in

Naples before Garibaldi should arrive. Nevertheless, the extraordinary success which had throughout attended the partisan chief threatened complications.

Garibaldi, left to himself, would inevitably shock the interests of France in Rome, precipitate a war with Austria in Venetia, and bring upon Italy the disapprobation of every court in Europe. His ultimate object was to cross the Alps to re-establish Hungary and Poland in the estimation of Europe, and there is little doubt that if these ends had been achieved the hopes and aspirations of Italian patriots would have been dashed to the ground. Few but Cavour realised the danger. On the 6th of September King Francis left Naples, on the next day Garibaldi entered, and before sunset the Italian flag was hoisted by the Neapolitan fleet.

While Garibaldi overran Sicily and Calabria, "flashing upon the effete system and spiritless armies of Neapolitan despotism like Æneas among the shades," public enthusiasm was concentrated on the hero, to the detriment of the statesman. It was felt that Garibaldi could inspire while Cavour could only control, and that the General was free from the taint of paltering with the self-interested friends of Italy. There was nothing left for Cavour, now that his first hopes were baffled, but to take up a strong line of action, and to send troops into Umbria and the Marches of Ancona. He used as a pretext the formation by the Pope of a mercenary army of foreigners for the purpose of maintaining his temporal power. He believed that by no other means could he prevent the forces of revolution from mastering the whole of Italy. Lamoricière, in command of the papal army, suffered reverse after reverse at the hands of the Piedmontese, and within three weeks from the time that Garibaldi had entered Naples Victor Emmanuel found himself master of Italy as far as the Abruzzi. "We are touching the supreme moment," Cavour cried in ecstasy; "with God's help Italy will be made in three months." Thus the bold step which he had undertaken had succeeded, and the further advance of irresponsible conquest was definitely checked. But his action at this crisis was so grave an infraction of the ordinary rules of international politics that Cavour thought it necessary to defend his conduct in a circular despatch sent to the various courts of Europe. He assured the world that he would never again summon French arms to his assistance, that the rumoured surrender to France of the island of Sardinia was not dreamt of, and that he would restrain Garibaldi from assaulting Venetia. The courts of Europe, with the exception of England, protested against his action, and the Pope produced the tarnished weapon of excommunication to terrorise the invaders of his dominion. Cavour was now resolved that a normal government should be established at Naples, and that Garibaldi should not go to Rome. It speaks much for his magnanimity that, when the King started on the march for Naples, Cavour implored his master to pay infinite regard to his brave opponent. "Garibaldi has become my most violent enemy," he declared, "but I desire for the good of Italy and the honour of your Majesty that he should retire entirely satisfied." Cavour's desire had always been that he should win independence without sacrificing liberty, and abolish monarchical absolutism without falling into revolutionary despotism. "I am the son of liberty, and to it I owe all that I am. If a veil is to be placed on its statue it is not for me to do it."

All was not yet accomplished. Garibaldi still opposed Cavour, and still held the dictatorship. Without hesitation Cavour invited the deputies to pass a Bill authorising the King's Government to accept the immediate annexation of such provinces of Central and Southern Italy as manifested by universal suffrage their desire to become an integral part of the constitutional monarchy of

Victor Emmanuel. Sicilian opinion itself was in favour of annexation. At length Garibaldi was forced to give way, and declared that if annexation was the will of the people he would consent to such a policy. On 26th October he met Victor Emmanuel at the little town of Teano. Without much parleying he yielded to the straightforward sense of the King, and forthwith retired to his home in the island of Caprera. By the month of November Cavour was able to affirm with impunity that the affairs of Naples and the Marches were purely Italian, and that the Powers of Europe had no business to meddle with them. The French fleet, at the urgent instigation of the English Government, was withdrawn in January of 1861, and on the 18th of February the first Italian Parliament assembled at Turin, and Victor Emmanuel assumed the title of King of Italy. On this being proclaimed Cavour resigned office, but he was called upon to return somewhat reluctantly by the King on the condition that the Ministry should be slightly modified. This new Ministry had now to determine their relations with the Vatican. Cavour was of the opinion that the Pope's domination as sovereign had ceased from the day when it was proved that it could not exist save by a double foreign occupation, but he felt strongly at the same time that without Rome

Italian unity would still be only a name. He believed that this problem was not only of vital importance to Italy, but also to two hundred thousand Roman Catholics in all parts of the globe; and that its solution ought not only to have a political, but also a moral and religious influence. He accordingly deliberately departed from his usual rule of letting things take their own course when he pledged himself and the monarchy to make "the Eternal City, on which rested twenty-five centuries of glory the splendid capital of the Italian kingdom." Believing that all depended on the sentiment of the people, he wished that the choice of the capital should be determined by high moral considerations. Rome seemed to unite all the conditions historical, intellectual, moral, which should form the capital of a great state, but he did not, however, allow himself to be carried away altogether by sentiment. It was obvious that the choice of Rome as the capital of a united Italy could only be made with the agreement of France, and on the strict understanding that the union of Rome and Italy should not be interpreted by the great mass of Catholics as the signal for the servitude of the Church. Cavour avowed that he was ready to promise the Holy Father that freedom which he had never obtained from those who called themselves his allies and devoted sons.

At Cavour's invitation then Parliament voted the choice of Rome as capital, but although so far successful Cavour failed to conclude a compact with the Vatican, and the state of the Neapolitan provinces continued to give him annoyance.

The subject of Rome being made the capital of a united Italy is closely concerned with Cavour's ecclesiastical policy, and it will not be out of place here to make a slight digression to study his opinions upon Church questions. To comprehend his attitude it must be remembered, in the first place, that Rome was not only defended by foreign arms, but it was also the seat of a power whose empire over the mind of man was not the sport of military or political vicissitudes. Therefore Cavour did not believe that the mere expulsion of the French troops would effect the incorporation of Rome into the kingdom of Italy. He for his part looked forward to a time when the Roman Catholic world would recognise that the Church could best fulfil its task in complete separation from temporal power, and this being accomplished, Rome would assume its natural position as the centre of the Italian State.

Now to demonstrate that Cavour carried out in practice what he was for ever preaching one incident will serve. He valued the independence of the Church so much that on the suppression of the

Piedmontese monasteries he refused to give to the State the administration of the revenue arising from the sale of their lands, and formed this into a fund belonging to the Church itself, in order that the clergy might not become the salaried officers of the State. He also tried to improve the condition and promote the independence of the lower clergy; to make them more national at heart. Whatever ecclesiastical views we may hold, it must be admitted that while Cavour claimed for Italy the whole of its national inheritance he determined to inflict no needless wound upon the conscience of Rome.

Cavour was not destined to survive his triumph long, for already the Angel of Death was nigh to rob Italy of the man who had contributed so much towards the great work of building up a united kingdom. Worn out and wearied with the clamour of political controversy, overstrained by the mass of his multifarious duties, in the month of May, of the year 1861, he fell seriously ill of a fever, which the physicians failed to subdue with their clumsy methods of bleeding. On the fourth day of his sickness he summoned a Cabinet Council to his bedside. Soon afterwards the King paid him a visit, and found him practically unconscious, and from that hour he became continually delirious. Some coherent sentiments, some coherent hopes on the theme which was ever nearest to his heart broke from him ever and anon, but on the 6th of June, as the grey dawn broke over the city, he passed away, a martyr to the cause which he had barely lived long enough to see successful.

Thus it was that Cavour lived and died for his country. There hardly ever was a cause that did not require its martyrs and was not founded on their sacrifice and cemented by their suffering. In this case Italian unity claimed the sacrifice and the suffering of one of the greatest statesmen whose name is to be found in the political annals of Europe.

When we study the character and the life story of those men who have made the world's history it is impossible not to conjure up in the mind some picture representative of the men we are studying. Such pictures must often prove ideal. We form an estimate of the character, the spirit of the man, and upon this framework we build up the flesh. To become thoroughly acquainted with the personal appearance of the great characters in history Carlyle himself believed to be essential to a correct understanding of their lives and dispositions.

"In all my poor historical investigations," he declares, " it is one of the most primary wants to procure a bodily likeness of the personage enquired after—a good portrait if such exists; failing that,

HIS PERSONAL APPEARANCE

even an indifferent if sincere one; in short, any representation made by a faithful human creature of that face and figure which he saw with his eyes, and which I can never see with mine. Often I have found the portrait superior in real instruction to half a dozen biographies, or rather, I have found that the portrait was as good as a small lighted candle by which the biographies could for the first time be read, and some human interpretation be made of them."

In appearance Cavour perhaps could hardly fulfil the expectations of those who have studied his character, if we are to judge from the endless statues and portraits that we encounter in Italy, but yet there was much in his features that gave token of the inner man. Always inclined to be stout, in later years he became somewhat ungainly. He stooped a little, and two narrow lines were visible on either side of a mouth cold and uneffusive, but although his features were not so striking as his character, a high and solid forehead gave the idea of power with which every one who came into contact with him was so much impressed, and his keen blue eyes, so changeful in expression, betokened a mind quick and alert to take in every detail around him. His carelessness in dress was proverbial, but in this alone could his bitterest enemies accuse him of negligence. His manners were simple, but distinguished by an unmistakably aristocratic ease and courtesy. He spoke generally low, without emphasis, and always appeared to pay the greatest attention to what was said to him, even by the least important person; a detail of character which, trifling as it may seem, constitutes one of the essentials of greatness.

"After a conversation with that man I breathe more freely, my mind dilates," declared one who had the privilege of an interview with Cavour, and it was in this power of transmitting his enthusiasm to others that lay the whole secret of his influence. But it must be owned that in Turin he often did not take sufficient pains to make himself agreeable, least of all to the King, and consequently was considered petulant and haughty by those who did not know him, arbitrary by those who did. In later years he underwent a change in this respect. He persuaded himself that no one was *ennuyeux*, and, acting upon this principle, he lived down the reputation of intolerance and arrogance that attached so unjustly to his name. Throughout his life he was possessed of a genial manner, the outcome of high animal spirits, which could only be checked by the depression of anxiety and overwork, and it was this liveliness of spirit, combined with strength of character, that endeared him to not a few, and exerted a powerful influence upon all his contemporaries. On the whole, then, the picture of his outward appearance is not altogether an unpleasing one, or unworthy of the man who gave to his country an organised force, a flag, a government, and foreign allies.

Perhaps the most interesting speculation on the career of Cavour concerns his relations with the two men who, after himself, were most instrumental in bringing about the union of the Italian kingdom. On the most cursory perusal of the main facts it is evident that sympathy between Cavour and Victor Emmanuel was always lacking, and yet both of them laid aside their personal feelings since they both knew that they were indispensable to each other in the great work which they were equally determined to complete. On his side the King looked to Cavour as to one who would lead to victory. Once he even went so far as to say that when driving with Cavour he felt just like the tenor who leads on the "prima donna" to receive applause. Cavour for his part declared with a loyalty, comparable only to that of Bismarck, that it was his creed that a single head should tower above all others, the head of the King; before him all subjects should bow down, any other attitude would be that of a rebel.

Thus it was that although Cavour had inflicted upon the King injuries which made it impossible for him to forgive his Minister in private, yet in public, when once a line of action had been determined upon they worked in faithful unison for the common cause. This attitude up to a certain point characterised his relations with Garibaldi, although the difference between the policy of the Statesman and the General was more marked than between the policy of the Statesman and the King. However, Cavour never changed his opinion of people, and even after the General had become his enemy he still admired and esteemed him. He never could forget, and indeed he was never slow to acknowledge the services that Garibaldi had rendered to Italy: "The greatest that a man could render her."

There are some who have maintained that it was not forbearance but fear that made Cavour relent in his relations with Garibaldi, but the truth of the matter is that he realised that Garibaldi stood as a great moral power, not only in Italy, but also in Europe. He recognised that if he entered into a quarrel with him European public opinion would be against him. The cession of Nice, the birthplace of Garibaldi, remained to the end the great bone of contention between the two men; but Cavour felt it as deeply as the other. He declared to the Chamber that an abyss had been created between himself and Garibaldi, that he had performed what he believed to have been a duty, but that it was the most cruel duty of his life.

Garibaldi himself was not so moderate. In writing to the King, when starting for Naples, he said that he would be proud to add to His Majesty's crown a new and perhaps more brilliant jewel, but only on the condition that His Majesty would stand opposed to councillors who would cede this province to a foreigner, as had been done with the city of his birth. In the famous debate of the 18th April 1861, Garibaldi publicly declared it would be for ever impossible for him to clasp the hand of the man who had sold his country to the foreigner. Cavour smarted under this blow, but with emotion replied, that if Garibaldi was unable to forgive him, he could not hold it to be a reproach to him. Throughout the controversy Cavour was determined that no private animosity should interfere with the help that Garibaldi could give him for the furthering of that cause to which he devoted his whole life. There is, in fact, nothing more remarkable, although it ought to go without saying, than Cavour's singleness of purpose. All his life was consecrated to one great work, the emancipation of his country. From the opening to the close of his public career the reflection, "I am an Italian citizen," governed his actions.

It has sometimes been affirmed, that it is comparatively easy for a determined man to become great if he has only one object to work for. It is the man with a versatile genius, the man who can do so many things with aptitude, who finds the path of life deviating and confusing. It is difficult for him to decide for what he is best suited, so many interests call him aside, now one way, now another, out of the straight course; whereas, the man with only one object in life, although he may fall far short of the other in talent and brilliance, succeeds where the other fails, because he perceives clearly his end, and makes for it, neither turning to the right nor to the left.

There is much truth in this statement, and it can be applied with effect to the career under consideration. Cavour saw the goal of his ambitions clearly, and to that end he strove throughout his life. As early as the year 1833 he was wont to dream that he was already Minister of the kingdom of Italy. Guizot once remarked that Cavour was the only man living who had an object, and who pursued it straightforwardly through every danger and every difficulty. But this determination to attain his ends by any means in due course laid him open to the charge of public immorality, from which no statesman of such a mould can be altogether free; and yet it has been well said that those alone are entitled to pass judgment on Cavour who have made a nation with purer hands. He has been called a pupil of the Machiavellian school, but he did not place such broad constructions upon Machiavelli's maxims as some others of his contemporaries have done. He believed that for a policy to be successful in Piedmont it should be unswerving in its aim; at the same time flexible and various as to the measures employed.

Moreover, if he was scrupulous about principles which he considered vital in dealing with men, and especially his colleague, d'Azeglio, he could not expect to avoid the suspicion of severe moralists. It is well known that Cavour looked upon Pitt as the *beau ideal* of the statesman, and yet Pitt bought rotten boroughs, and by being prodigal of places, honours, pensions, he obtained a majority. He believed that in this Pitt was not wrong because he loved power, not as an end but as a means to an end. Cavour believed that the union of England and Ireland was for the good of both countries. He condemned the members of the Irish Parliament who were bribed to vote for the union, but he did not equally condemn the government, which purchased these corrupt men, because he believed in public opinion, and he knew that public opinion had at all times treated with indulgence the immoral acts which had brought about great political results, and had sanctioned in government the use of a different morality from that binding on individuals. His worst enemies, however, cannot accuse Cavour of loving power for power's sake. He was ambitious, but what great man is not possessed of ambition? "I own I am ambitious," he once said, "enormously ambitious, and when I am Minister I hope I shall justify my ambition," yet with it all, he cared nothing for power as power, but only as a means to compass the good of his country. Like Bismarck, he desired the substance of power, not the shadow, and it can be said of him with truth, that he never purchased power at the cost of those principles which he declared were part of himself.

The two qualities that distinguished the personality of Cavour, from the very beginning, were his vigour and determination; the essential complement of greatness. The vacillating and hesitating man can never be truly great. The man who is always led by another, who fears the opinion of his neighbours, and who truckles to public opinion, can never, under any circumstances, win success. Courage and determination enabled Cavour to carry out the great purpose of his life. Early in his career, he declared that if ever he came to be Minister, he would resign or effect the triumph of his principles. In the face of any present obstacle, an invincible confidence came over him in his power to surmount it. He believed that determination was a sure road to triumph, and he was patient enough to perceive that failure was only a by-road to success. Cavour once gave a clever demonstration of his methods, which is best told in his own words.

"I see the straight line to that point. Supposing that halfway I encounter an impediment, I do not knock my head against it, for the pleasure of breaking it, but neither do I go back. I look to the right, and to the left, and not being able to follow the straight line I make a curve. I turn the obstacle which I cannot attack in front."

With this simple demonstration it is not difficult to understand his methods, and that which made his determination still more effective was a certain degree of caution, that tempered all his actions. Manzoni said of him, that he had all a statesman's prudence. With a miraculous power of instantly grasping a new situation, he would take care to do nothing rash, although he was ever inclined to think that in all serious contingencies to act is better than not to act, and consequently he never incurred the charge of excessive caution. His methods of diplomacy were scarcely conventional. In delicate negotiations his maxim was to say only what he thought. As to the habit attributed to diplomatists of disguising their thoughts it was one of which he never availed himself, because he flattered himself that he had found out the art of deceiving diplomatists. His original method was to speak the truth, and he was then certain that no one would believe him. The result appears to have been excellent. Metternich called him the only diplomatist in Europe. Without going so far as to admit this, it cannot be denied that throughout the anxious period preceding the outbreak of the war he exhibited all the necessary qualities of a diplomatist; patience, temper, forethought, resource, and resolution. He ever showed great ability in compelling the most various and opposing elements to combine in the service of his ends; and yet with all this he never gave a thought to the consequence of a phrase uttered in a moment of gaiety, discouragement or confidence.

It is curious that with so much ability and talent Cavour was never a very proficient writer or speaker. "You must expect no article from me," he himself wrote at the time when he had taken to journalism, "demanding any expenditure of imagination. I was never able to compose the simplest tale to amuse my nephew, although I have often tried. I must confine myself therefore to matters of pure reason." He therefore never strove after brilliancy of effect, but wrote with a particular purpose, with the unfortunate result that his articles appear to us devoid of attraction. His speaking, like his writing, was commonplace; yet it was plain, argumentative, and to the purpose. He had no formed style, no graces or tricks of elocution. His delivery it seems was difficult, broken and painful to listen to, and it was more the matter than the manner that impressed and convinced his audience. In the way of preparation he did no more than think over the subject, and arrange his ideas, trusting to the inspiration of the moment for words and phrases.

For the rest, it may be mentioned, that Cavour was not appreciative of art or poetry. He took pleasure in reading Shakespeare, but the pleasure he experienced was not derived from any scientific knowledge of rhythm or metre. The splendid monuments and art treasures of Rome did not seem to appeal to him in the least degree. At any rate, if he did appreciate the beauties of nature and art, he took great pains to conceal the fact. It might be said that hard work was his only hobby. Always a great worker, towards the end of his life he allowed his studies and business to interfere with his rest and refreshment. He took but a small allowance of sleep, and latterly, only partook of one hearty meal in the day. D'Azeglio said of Cavour that he was possessed of a diabolical activity. In his religious protestations he was probably sincere. He looked up to his religion as a great moralising force, and found comfort, like many of the great men of history, in the submitting to the ruling of a superior will, regarding his devotions, as the outward and visible sign of this submission. But Cavour was not without his faults. He himself owned to a fondness for gambling. He even feared that "the humiliating and degrading emotions of play," to use his own words, threatened to undermine his intellectual and moral faculties; but it can be taken for granted that he overstimated the danger. Cavour rarely listened to advice, and only took it when it happened to coincide with his own opinions. Again, he was reputed to be inordinately extravagant. He entertained the profoundest contempt for small economies, and acted upon the principle of "being robbed without saying a word."

With one limitation it can be said that his character was peculiarly devoid of the minor vices to which the flesh is generally heir, considering the circumstances in which he lived. Nothing can excuse his acquiescence in the marriage of the Princess Clotilde, daughter of his King, to one of the most odious of mankind. In this instance he made the great mistake of allowing political convenience to outweigh private individual considerations; but even this grave error of judgment is condoned by a life devoted exclusively to the service of his country. To quote a striking passage in Hayward's essay on Cavour in the *Edinburgh Review*:

"He had none of the qualities which we have been led by melancholy experiences to regard as the inevitable alloy of greatness: neither the theatrical arts of Chatham, nor the cold cruel impassibility to groans and tears of Richelieu, nor the cynic contempt for principle of Frederick, nor the revolting hypocrisy of Cromwell, nor the desolating selfishness of Napoleon. His ambition, made of purer, holier stuff, was merged and forgotten in his patriotism. His statesmanship was reason and truth put in action, and therefore it is that his example may prove of inestimable value to posterity."

The influence of Cavour upon Italy has been

compared, not without some justification, to that of Napoleon I. in France. Just as Napoleon was no genuine Frenchman, so Cavour was no genuine Italian in mind or temperament, or even in accent, and they were both the stronger for this diversity. Beneath a cold and impassable exterior there was room for an undergrowth of political virtues, hardly understood in Italy, and nothing but his solidity and indomitable power of resistance could have withstood the shocks which his versatility could not always avoid. Lord Palmerston said that Cavour left a name "to point a moral and adorn a tale," and perhaps this short sentence best describes his greatness, and best explains the affection which most Italians feel for his memory. The worship of Cavour is the worship of an idea, and that idea is the union of Italy, for which he, above all others, was actively responsible. Cavour has left behind him a renown for patriotism, personal disinterestedness, and an ambition honourably directed that will survive to the latest period in the annals of his native land.

PART III
BISMARCK

It has always been held inexpedient to discuss the actions or to estimate the greatness of any man who has attained to a conspicuous place in the service of his country, until a sufficient interval has elapsed after his death; both in virtue of the fact that the time may not yet have come when the rash and indiscriminate judgments which contempories are wont to pass on his actions can be calmly reviewed in the light of subsequent history, and that a large amount of evidence, which may be essential to a judicious estimation of his character, it will be imperative to omit. His biographers accordingly find themselves glossing over many of his conspicuous faults, out of due consideration to his colleagues and relatives who may still be living, or making light of his virtues to suit the antagonistic opinions of his contemporary opponents. Thus we find that until his generation has passed away, it is only possible to arrive at a compromise of the truth. But this generalisation seems not to be applicable in the case of Bismarck. No decent interval has been allowed to elapse after his death, before the publication of a large mass of private correspondence and documents, having immediate bearing upon his character and his achievements. Bismarck, in conversation one day with Busch, his biographer, said: " When once I am dead you can tell everything you like, absolutely everything you know."

As a statesman and as a diplomatist his character has consequently been made so plain to us that there is very little to wait for before giving our final judgments. Almost every word from his lips or his pen found its way to publicity; either during his lifetime or soon after his death. It is not probable that the present generation, or any other that is to come, will understand the motives that inspired him, the ideals that sustained him, and the reasons for his policies, any better than we do to-day. The almost idolatrous veneration of his countrymen has made it possible to reveal much in connection with his name, which is of such a nature that, if a similar course had been adopted with regard to certain of his contemporaries, it would have been condemned as indiscreet and mischievous.

The truth of the matter is that the German

people as a whole held his name in such reverence that they became insensible to his demerits, and, while they ignored all that was defective in his character, attributed his political errors to the irresistible force of circumstances, and entertained no scruple in giving publication to his most questionable actions, construing all good or bad to be for the lasting welfare of his fatherland. His faults, then, are either excused or forgotten, owing to the willing credulity and enthusiastic veneration which the most discerning of his countrymen agree to pay to the nation's idol. In the art of inspiring large masses of human beings with confidence and attachment hardly any statesman has surpassed him, and he acquired a popularity which few have more merited, and to which still fewer have attained. The result has been welcome to the biographers of this generation, as there is now within the reach of all much material of vital importance to any history of the nineteenth century. Doubtless the more sober judgment of future historians will not permit an excess of enthusiasm to bias a criticism of Bismarck's career. The attempts to whitewash his character and to slur over his shortcomings will become more and more futile, but whatever subsequent history may have in store for its final verdict, posterity will never be able to deny that the most remarkable feature in Bismarck's character was the immutability of purpose, the unflinching and unsparing energy with which he devoted himself to his great life-work.

The story of his public career will stand for all time as a conspicuous example of a statesman who, by an indomitable force of will, hacked his way through all opposition, fearless of unpopularity and heedless of the limitations imposed by conventional moralists, while it will ever be remembered that he earned his great and enduring reputation by means of eminent services rendered to his country. Future historians then, while they must justifiably lay stress upon his faults for the benefit of those patriots whose hysterical enthusiasm blinds them to the truth, will pay a high tribute of honour to the man, who, having set himself a stupendous task, succeeded in freeing his country from extraneous influence, and giving to it that strength which can only be derived from union.

Bismarck was born on the 1st of April 1815 at Schönhausen in Brandenburg. Of his childhood and youth little is known, a circumstance which can hardly be regretted, seeing that it is a common error on the part of biographers to attach unwarrantable significance to the recorded sayings and doings of youth which, even if they can be credited, with few exceptions are valueless in their bearings on the subsequent career. It is sufficient here to notice that before he was nineteen years of age he entered the University of Göttingen. Eschewing the prevalent taste for philosophy he turned his attention to history, a sound knowledge of which is generally considered to be an essential part of a statesman's outfit. In his youth he justly earned a reputation for wild living, but even during this *jeunesse orageuse* his mind perpetually turned upon politics, and he often puzzled his boon companions by starting at the midnight supper table political monologues of interminable length.

In 1835 he took the degree of Doctor of Law at the Berlin University, and at this point it seemed as if his career was to come to a standstill. At first he wished to settle down to the steady pursuits of a country gentleman on his father's estate, and not to venture upon the quicksands of politics, but the decisions of the Congress at Vienna had aroused his interest in current events, and formulated in his mind some very definite views on the European situation. To these views he gave violent expression in occasional speeches, which earned for him the reputation of holding ultra-loyalist views, and as early as the year 1847 it was prophesied that in the young Bismarck had arisen a new Otto of Saxony who would do all for his country that his great namesake had achieved eight hundred years before. There seemed at the time little chance of the prophecy being fulfilled, as after his marriage he returned to Schönhausen with a view to settling down once again as a country squire. From his retirement, however, Bismarck was aroused by the mighty wave of revolution, which in the year 1848 moved in a series of concentric circles over the face of Europe.

It was this great disturbance that made Bismarck, as it made Cavour. But for the present events of that year were a cruel blow to his monarchical pride, and his political sagacity recognised the necessity of yielding to accomplished facts. He regarded the whole movement as so much midsummer madness, and throughout remained faithful to monarchical authority as the one thing needful for the Prussian State. While the German people were spreading broadcast their new-fangled notions of liberty, the voice of the young ultra-loyalist was uplifted against a movement which seemed to threaten the humbling of that monarchy which he regarded as the sacred inviolable symbol of order and good governance. Loyalist he was in excess.

It has been truly said that no churchman of

the dark ages ever believed more devoutly in the divine virtue of the consecrating oil. He was one of the two deputies who refused to join in the vote of thanks to Frederick William IV. for the constitution which he had promised to Prussia. Bismarck therefore did not for a while seek election to the new assembles, both because he perceived that they were being republicanised, and because he refused to believe that Prussia required regenerating. At the same time it was not in his nature to stand aside while the Prussian King was weakly subjecting himself to the will of an alien Parliament. Soliciting the co-operation of Kleist and Von Bülow, two kindred spirits, he organised an aristocratic party which he determined, even if the King's support failed him, should make its presence felt and serve as a counterpoise to the revolutionary spirit. These courageous and enterprising men met frequently at the house of Bismarck's father-in-law, and with their combined efforts published a journal known as the *Kreuz Zeitung*, which attracted the attention and roused the hostility of the dominant Liberals and revolutionary parties. For a while Bismarck exerted every means in his power to influence the vacillating King, but with scant success, although the overthrow of the revolutionary government by the army in Vienna told in his favour, as the King of Prussia now entertained hopes of a similar triumph in Berlin. For the present, however, the King refused to put complete reliance upon Bismarck, whom he regarded as a reactionary "who smelt of blood, and who would be more useful on a future occasion."

When Bismarck made up his mind to offer his candidature for the New Assembly he called upon the electors to aid him in his efforts to restore confidence between the crown and the people. Reaction had already set in over Europe, so that his utterances in the Assembly carried with them some influence. He made it his special mission to hinder all attempts of the majority to model a new constitution on the constitution of some foreign country. In particular he refused to countenance the example afforded by England. He always regarded the English Reform Bill as a national fiasco, threatening the prosperity of a country which owed its greatness, not to a democratic, but to an aristocratic constitution. Nor were his asseverations merely the outcome of an aristocratic prejudice "sucked in with his mother's milk." What he feared above all things was that a political experiment might ruin the prospects of Prussia. He vigorously upheld the doctrine that the Prussian nobles had been the truest defenders of the State, while he believed it to be a vulgar error to confuse patriotism and Liberalism. He was withal a thorough Royalist, the type of the rough and masterful squire to whom all reforms were hateful, and in this capacity he continued to take a prominent part in the Parliaments of Berlin and Erfurt, where two grave problems were awaiting solution. In the first place, there was the Austrian question to come under immediate consideration. It must be remembered that an appreciable section of Germany was included in the Austrian Empire, and since the Assembly was unable to coerce the Austrian Empire, it was deemed advisable that the rest of Germany should be reconstituted and the Austrian provinces eliminated; an arrangement which the Austrian Government was not disposed to accept. In the second place, there was the relation between the individual states and the new Central Authority to be discussed.

The title of German Emperor was offered to the King of Prussia, but he declined, on the plea that he could only accept the honour from his equals the German princes, in which determination he was supported by Bismarck, who with some significance declared that the gold which gave truth to the brilliance of the crown of Frankfort had first to be won by melting down the Prussian crown. His motto was, " Prussians we are and Prussians we will remain." The only means of coercing the princes seemed to be to rely on the Prussian army, and Bismarck saw clearly that there was only one policy for Prussia to pursue. Peace must be maintained with Austria while the Prussian army should be gaining in strength and efficiency.

In 1851 Bismarck was sent as the representative of Prussia to the restored Diet of Frankfort, where he at once found himself in a maze of diplomatic negotiations. He complained bitterly that his relations with others were those of mutual suspicion and espionage, and he was obliged to acquire the art of "saying nothing in many words." In earlier days he had looked upon Austria as the mainstay of monarchical order, but now he perceived that Austria was a power that meant to rule in Germany uncontrolled. He found a cunning and arrogant enemy, where he had looked to find a genial and steadfast friend, and before he had been in Frankfort a year he had discovered that this hostility was practically insurmountable.

At Frankfort for the first time in his life he saw Prussia as others saw her, and it was a bitter disillusion to him to find that she looked less like a planet ruling a firmament of her own than a satellite of Austria, gravitating with the rest of the German States in her rival's orbit; and yet he saw that Prussia, being exclusively a German State had a prior claim to be the authoritative exponent of a German national policy. Finally, he pronounced the so-called federal system to be a mere device for employing the secondary German States for the aggrandisement of Austria and the humiliation of Prussia. With these convictions he quickly made up his mind as to the proper course to be pursued.

The hypothesis being that Austria was now the enemy of Prussia, the conclusion was that Prussia must oppose Austria by diplomacy or war. Prussia was obviously not strong enough to do so alone, and since Bismarck scorned to seek aid from the other German States he was constrained to look abroad for allies. Russia and France must both be sounded. One, or better, both, must be solicited for their aid. Prussia must have the upper hand in German affairs, and Austria must be isolated. "We must look abroad for allies," he declared, "and among the European Powers Russia is to be had on the cheapest terms; it wishes only to grow in the East, the other two at our expense." He believed that if only Prussia would come to an understanding with the Czar the other German States would turn to Prussia for support, not wishing to be dragged into a war to help Austria.

Bismarck's behaviour at Frankfort considerably enhanced his reputation as a diplomatist, and he was now frequently summoned to Berlin that his advice might be taken. In 1854 France wished for an alliance with Austria, but Austria dared not move without the support of Prussia and Germany, so that by means of Bismarck's diplomatic manœuvres matters had come to such a pass that a question of European importance rested with the King of Prussia for decision. Bismarck was now summoned to Berlin to give his opinion.

The advice he proffered was to hold the balance of Europe. He wished to frighten Austria by threatening an alliance with Russia, and at the same time to frighten the Czar by making him think that Prussia was joining the Western Powers. The plan of campaign was "to retain the possibility of threatening to decide with Russia," but unfortunately the King was wavering between the Czar and Louis Napoleon, and no sooner had Bismarck left Berlin than a treaty was made to support the Austrian demands. Bismarck's behaviour on this occasion bears testimony to his self-control and loyalty. The only comment to which he committed himself was equivocal enough. "The King has as much leniency for the sins of Austria as I hope to have from the Lord in heaven." He was convinced that Prussia ought to assert a national policy wholly independent of the court of Vienna, and it may well be imagined that he was now thoroughly disgusted with the action of Frederick William. Nothing daunted, he turned his attention to an alliance with Louis Napoleon, but the general feeling in Germany was that such a course would be mean. This much he was ready to admit, but in support of his ideas he made the characteristic observation, "Very admirable people, even German princes in the Middle Ages, have used a sewer to make their escape rather than be beaten or throttled."

After the Crimean War circumstances seemed to favour his French policy. The Emperor desired a union with Prussia, so that in the year 1857, Bismarck found himself in Paris making overtures. It was obvious that an alliance with France would be advantageous, because Austria was the natural enemy of Prussia, and if Prussia repelled the advances of Louis Napoleon he would no doubt seek an alliance with the Czar, but the King still urged that France was the natural enemy of Germany; that Louis Napoleon was the representative of revolution, and that therefore there could be no true and lasting union between a King of Prussia and an Emperor of the French. In 1857, however, the health of the King broke down, and a decree was signed appointing his brother as Regent. A few months considerably developed the situation.

Early in the following year Louis Napoleon and Cavour came to an understanding to drive the Austrians out of Italy, and the Prince Regent, deeming that the time for a decisive policy had arrived, placed the Prussian army on a war footing, offering the Emperor of Austria his armed neutrality and a guarantee of the Austrian possessions in Italy. In return he requested to have the command of all forces of the German Diet, but Austria, refusing his assistance, made peace with France.

Bismarck at this crisis was sent to St Petersburg, much to his chagrin, as Russia was not playing an important part in these European complications. It was a critical period in his career. In addition to his mental depression he suffered severely from physical ailment, and the combination produced in him for the moment a callous indifference to the state of the momentous questions at issue. To use his own words he threatened to wrap himself up in his bearskin and be snowed up, and if that would not do he should go to earth and have done with politics. Meanwhile at home General Von Roon, a strong Conservative, and a man of considerable energy, had been appointed Minister of War, and his appointment was the signal for a new departure in home and foreign politics.

Bismarck at this time had no influence on home affairs, but he could have had no better friend in power than Von Roon, seeing that Von Roon wished for a Conservative Ministry with Bismarck, who was alone ready and willing to undertake the reform of the army as its President. In 1861 Bismarck's opportunities seemed within measurable distance. The Ministry had refused to allow the King to celebrate his accession by receiving the solemn homage of his people, and Von Roon on this and similar accounts wrote to summon Bismarck to Berlin. "If the King will to some extent meet my views, then I will set to work with pleasure," was Bismarck's characteristic reply, but the King still held back, and a compromise was effected between the Ministry and the Crown. This arrangement, however, did not hinder the King from asking the advice of Bismarck, who used his utmost endeavours to persuade the King to adopt a bolder line of policy. His solicitations proved too hazardous, and his appointment as Foreign Minister was accordingly postponed. At this period of his life no one took him seriously. He was forming his great schemes openly, and with a lightheartedness which those who met him mistook for insincerity. He wished in fact to be thought insincere, because when the time came for action he could carry out his plan or he could drop it without the charge of inconsistency which more serious statesmen were perpetually incurring; but for him these were years of self-education in which were sown the seeds of all his future achievements.

The next elections revealed a defeat for the Conservative party, and there now remained two alternatives for the King: either he must abandon the army problem, or he must govern against the will of the majority in the Chamber. Bismarck arrived in Berlin four days after the elections. All those who wished to perpetuate the authority of the Crown looked to him as their natural leader, but he did not wish to enter the Ministry except as Foreign Minister, and the King still feared and distrusted him. Accordingly it was decided that he should go as Minister to Paris.

Soon after his appointment he paid a visit to England where he met Disraeli, to whom he confided his determination, that whenever it was possible for him to undertake the leadership of the Prussian Government he would re-organise the army with or without the help of Parliament.

The opportunity to put his theories into practice arrived sooner than he might have expected.

In September the House by a large majority refused to vote the money for army reform. The King stuck to his guns at this crisis, calculating that it would be impossible for him to carry on the Government, in spite of the asseverations of the Ministers, who declared that they would support him to the end. Von Roon promptly stepped forward and advised the King to appoint Bismarck as Minister President, which advice the King accepted. Bismarck, in response to the call, hurried to Potsdam, where he found the King seated at a table with an Act of Abdication already signed lying before him. To his eternal credit he made haste to assure the King that he was willing to undertake the government without a Budget, and without a majority. The Act of Abdication accordingly became waste paper, and Bismarck was appointed Foreign Minister. Thus it was that the destinies of Prussia fell into the hands of the three men who were thoroughly at one in their aim—the enforcement of Prussia's ascendancy by means of the army.

Once possessed of power, Bismarck acquired a great influence over his sovereign, but his personal characteristics, his arrogance, his sarcasm and habit of banter, exasperated the members of the Chamber.

He failed altogether to make his purpose and his motives intelligible to the representatives of the Prussian people. In his new post he made a series of speeches, chiefly remarkable for their wealth of caustic wit and epigram. It is noteworthy that he was guilty of the common error which so often vitiates the preliminary efforts of young and aspiring statesmen.

There is a belief prevalent among youthful orators that well-turned sentences and epigrammatic conceits are the only essentials of public speaking. The maturer judgment of the experienced debater discerns that so far from being essential, these are superfluous or even dangerous, and although such intellectual garnish may for a time serve to deceive an audience and successfully veneer over the dry rot that may lie beneath, the most lenient of critics will soon discern its superficial nature.

Nevertheless, during these debates Bismarck gave utterance to some sentences which will be remembered so long as the German language lasts. It was in the course of one of his first oratorical efforts that he let slip the memorable words which gave earnest of his future policy: "The boundaries of Prussia are not those of a sound State. Not by speeches and majority of votes are the great questions of the time decided—that was the blunder of 1848 and 1849—but by blood and iron."

III.]   THE POLICY OF BLOOD AND IRON   161

These words have been justifiably misinterpreted. Bismarck in after years was constrained to explain them in public: "Put the strongest military power into the hands of the King of Prussia, then you will be able to carry out the policy you wish; it cannot be done with speeches and celebrations and songs; it can only be done by blood and iron." But it was shots such as this driven home with such frank brutality that caused the popular assembly to look upon him as a mere bully and absolutist of the old type, and so embittered the struggle that reconciliation between the Ministers and the Chamber was well-nigh an impossibility.

The session closed when the House of Lords threw out the Budget in its amended form. Bismarck insisted that, in the event of a disagreement between the two Houses, the Crown was still possessed of its absolute authority, so that the actual contest turned really on the issue who was to rule Prussia—the Hohenzollerns or Parliament? Nothing could shake the King's confidence in his Minister and he was resolved upon carrying out his military reforms in the face of all opposition; but unfortunately at this time internal disputes were swallowed up in the universal anxiety caused by the revolt of the Poles against the Russian Government. This disturbance for a while proved a stumbling-block to Bismarck who was endeavouring to isolate Austria by keeping on good terms with England and France. Since these two countries had remonstrated with the Czar it was imperative for Bismarck to quarrel either with Russia or France, and by way of an overture the King had written to the Czar proposing that the two governments should take common steps to meet the common danger. The progressive majority in the Parliament of Berlin thereupon accused Bismarck of isolating Prussia in Germany and in Europe, but, despite the vociferations of his opponents, he refused to leave the position he had taken up.

Pouring contempt upon that characteristic German romanticism which gave birth to so much enthusiasm for the welfare of other nations, he asserted that it was the duty of Germany to use all the power of the State to destroy the Polish language and nationality; that the Poles in Prussia must become Prussians as those in Russia had to become Russians. As a matter of fact Bismarck had established a closer relation between the courts of Berlin and St Petersburg than had existed any time since the commencement of the regency, and secured for Prussia a degree of confidence on the part of the Czar which in the memorable years that were to follow served it scarcely less effectually than an armed alliance, with the result that, when events occurred which opened to Prussia the road to political fortune, Bismarck received his reward in the liberty of action given him by the Russian Government. Moreover, Bismarck had given further proof of his diplomatic genius at this crisis in refusing to entertain the Czar's tempting proposal of a joint attack on France and Austria, perceiving that in the event of such a contingency Prussia would sacrifice much during the war, and obtain little or no compensation when peace was made. He openly declared that France would regard Prussia as a valuable ally when Prussia should have absorbed a minor state or two. At present the configuration of Prussia was impossible, "She wants belly on the side of Cassel and Nassau, her shoulder is out of joint on the side of Hanover: she is *en l'air*, and this painful situation condemns her to follow implicitly the policy of Vienna and St Petersburg, to revolve unceasingly in the orbit of the Holy Alliance."

Bismarck's truculent attitude and the general friction caused by the grave international crisis necessitated a closing of the session. No sooner had the session been closed than a series of ordinances was published by royal proclamation, creating stringent regulations for the control of the press, which did not enhance the popularity of the King. A serious breach seemed imminent between court and country, and to render the situation more hopeless dissensions had arisen within the court itself. The Crown Prince, influenced by his English sympathies and the opinion of the English court which was strongly unfavourable to Bismarck, after in vain protesting against a policy of violence which endangered his own prospective interests in the Crown, definitely declared himself against the Government. This circumstance would not have created so much mischief had it not been that the *Times* newspaper unfortunately procured some correspondence which had passed between the King and his son. The attitude that was adopted by the Crown Prince in these letters greatly increased Bismarck's aversion to what he considered to be English influence, and widened the breach between himself and the Liberal party. Now, the Liberal party looked forward to the early death of the King, who was advancing in years, fondly believing that ere long they would have it all their own way; but the King did not die, and the old conflict continued.

It has often been alleged that Bismarck deliberately maintained the friction in order to make himself indispensable. This was undoubtedly the case, but, after all, he was only adopting methods which have generally been employed by those who have sufficient discernment to realise that they will gain their ends if only their opponents are allowed to blunder on long enough. That Parliament was in opposition to Bismarck was to him an advantage, as he was not therefore beholden to it in any way, and so long as he maintained his almost unbounded influence over the King he felt comparatively secure. But now an international difficulty arose which seemed to threaten his ascendancy at court and his influence in the country. This was the Schleswig-Holstein question. Of this question it has been said that Machiavellism in its boldest flights has never produced anything parallel to it, and Bismarck was the great moving spirit of all the negotiations and disputes that were involved.

To confine an exceedingly lengthy and complicated story within due limits it is only necessary to touch upon the more vital points in the history of this European dispute. The union of the Duchies of Schleswig and Holstein with the Danish crown dated from the year 1460, Holstein forming part of the Holy Roman Empire, Schleswig not being so bound, although allied to Holstein. All attempts at absolute incorporation with Denmark had failed previous to the crucial year 1848. Frederick VII. who succeeded at this time to the throne of Denmark yielded to the so-called Eider-Danish party who aimed at making the river Eider the boundary of the Danish kingdom, and deliberately drew up a constitution for the whole realm, including the two Duchies. The inhabitants of Schleswig thereupon made a vigorous protest against their incorporation with Denmark, and in Holstein feeling was hardly less bitter. Popular enthusiasm in Germany ran high in favour of the obstinate Duchies, but with this enthusiasm Bismarck felt little sympathy as he did not wish the Holsteiners to live peacefully under the government of a Duke, ceasing, as they would, to take interest in Prussia. What Bismarck intended was that Schleswig-Holstein, itself incorporated more or less directly with Prussia, should be made the means of the destruction of the existing federal system and of the expulsion of Austria from Germany, and with incomparable resolution he bore down all opposition of people and courts, and forced a reluctant nation to the goal which he had himself chosen for it.

In 1863 King Frederick VII. died, but Christian of Glücksburg, who succeeded him, was obliged to sign the Constitution, which, added to the fact that the Duke of Augustenburg now came forward claiming his succession to the disputed Duchy, revived the whole question anew. The German people, including the Crown Prince, demanded with one voice of Bismarck that he should acknowledge the new duke, but for the present he merely made great profession of outraged honour, declaring that "honour as well as wisdom allows us to leave no doubt as to our loyalty to our engagements."

Wisdom doubtless had more weight with Bismarck on this occasion than honour, as he knew full well that if the King complied with the wishes of the German people he would have arrayed against him Denmark, Russia, and England with her fleet; whereas, if he opposed the claims of the Duke of Augustenburg these countries, most probably with France as well, would give him their support against the combined weight of German public opinion, the German Diet, and the Prussian Parliament, which, by the way, he neither respected nor feared. So he publicly complained that he was the scapegoat of German opinion, although privately the fact troubled him but little. He was pursuing, he affirmed, the course which he believed to be beneficial to his country and to Germany with a perfectly easy conscience. As to the means, he would use those within his reach in default of better.

He once remarked to the Crown Prince that he would not care if he were hung, provided the rope used for his execution would bind the new Germany to the throne, but in spite of all his patriotic protestations the Lower Chamber refused the supplies which he demanded for operations in the Duchies, and formally resolved to resist his policy by every means at its command.

The resistance of Parliament and of the Diet were alike unavailing against this master of diplomacy. Bismarck managed to secure the co-operation of Austria, in spite of his previous enmity with the Court of Vienna, by representing the agitation in the minor states in favour of the Duke of Augustenburg as a revolutionary one, and, by appealing to the memories of 1848, to awe the Emperor's advisers into direct concert with the Court of Berlin as the representative of monarchical order, in defiance of the wish of all the rest of Germany and of the demands of his own subjects. Perhaps this manœuvre of Bismarck constitutes the most consummate piece of diplomacy that the history of the world records. In February Bismarck was able to deliver an ultimatum at Copenhagen demanding the repeal of the November Constitution, and on its rejection he had the supreme satisfaction of triumphantly conducting the re-modelled

Prussian army into the field in alliance with Austria.

The English Government at this juncture proposed a conference, but Bismarck, at the suggestion of Louis Napoleon, who was on no friendly terms with England, set about the annexation of the Duchies to Prussia. His first plan was to convince England that Denmark could not retain the Duchies. Austria he knew preferred that they should belong to Prussia rather than to Augustenburg. Failing to annex the Duchies, his second scheme was to acquire Kiel for the Prussian navy and to engineer a canal through Holstein so that Prussian ships might reach the North Sea without passing through the Sound.

In May, Bismarck accorded the Duke of Augustenburg an interview. What passed between the two men is uncertain, but conclusions may be drawn from the fact that, after it had taken place, Bismarck sent off despatches to St Petersburg, Paris and London intimating that he was not disposed to support Augustenburg in the future, and instructing ambassadors to act in accordance with this decision. His subsequent behaviour was indeed characteristic of the man. The Czar having now brought forward a new candidate in the person of the Duke of Oldenberg,

Bismarck declared that he was ready to support him. This he did, not because he had any serious intention of fulfilling such an engagement, but because he would by this means gain a double advantage in conciliating the Czar and postponing a settlement of the affair by producing another candidate to contest the Duchy.

Such action must be considered unscrupulous or not according to the elasticity of our moral codes, but there are few who can deny that by his next move he overstepped all the limits of public spirit and integrity. He published in the Prussian newspapers an assertion that the Duke of Augustenburg had intimated to him in the course of his private interview that he had never asked the Prussians for help, and that he could get on very well without their assistance. Augustenburg, it is practically certain, never said anything of the kind, but at any rate this breach of confidence produced the desired effect, and served Bismarck's purpose to prejudice the King of Prussia against the prince.

Now, since the conference in London had proved unproductive of any definite conclusion Bismarck was left with a free hand to deal with Denmark, and a brilliant victory of the Prussian arms forced the enemy to capitulate. By the Treaty of Vienna in October 1864 King Christian ceded his rights in the whole of Schleswig-Holstein to the sovereigns of Austria and Prussia jointly, but it must be understood that Bismarck had entered the dispute entirely in the interests of Germany centred at Berlin and ruled by the House of Hohenzollern. That Austria would not without compensation permit the Duchies to fall completely under Prussian sway was well known to Bismarck, but so far from causing him any hesitation in his policy he was pleased to discern in the Schleswig-Holstein question a favourable pretext for the war which was to drive Austria out of Germany.

Bismarck announced at Vienna on the 22nd February 1865 the terms in which he declared his willingness that Schleswig-Holstein should be conferred by the two sovereigns on Frederick of Augustenburg, but they were terms that Austria could not accept, and war now seemed inevitable between the two rival powers. Bismarck wanted if possible to avoid war for the present, as he was of the opinion that the Prussian army was not yet prepared for it. No one knew better than Bismarck how to strike when the iron was hot, and no one knew better than he the moment when it was hot enough to mould according to his own pattern. The development of the European situation made it advisable to postpone the rupture. Austria now found herself on the horns of a dilemma. Italy threatened her on one side while Prussia threatened her on the other, so an agreement was patched up at Gastein. The Duchy of Lauenberg was to be handed over to the King of Prussia, who was also to administer Schleswig, and Austria was to manage the affairs of Holstein. This settlement was only a temporary expedient, but Prussia had come out of the affair with flying colours, whereas Austria had suffered a blow to her prestige in the eyes of the other German states.

Put briefly, Bismarck's part in the Schleswig-Holstein dispute was this. Having made Austria his catspaw in occupying the Duchies with a view to an equal division, he suddenly turned round upon her, claimed, and eventually appropriated both, and then had sown the seeds of that conflict with Austria which he considered essential for the consolidation of the German Empire. But for the present his preparations were incomplete. After the treaty had been arranged he visited Louis Napoleon, from which interview he concluded that the Emperor was prepared to offer him the Duchies, but as the interview was held without a witness it is difficult to know for certain what passed between the two. Bismarck seems to have convinced the Emperor that it was in the interest of France to encourage Prussia in the ambitious fulfilment of her national duty. In other words he secured French neutrality. Louis Napoleon in after years declared that Bismarck had promised some recompense in return, but if this was the case he certainly took no steps to carry his promise into effect.

It was on his return from Biarritz that Bismarck grimly remarked: "If Italy did not exist we should be obliged to invent her," but when he turned his attention to Italy he found it was more difficult to deal with the Italians than with Louis Napoleon. They distrusted Bismarck because they feared that he would allow them to be dragged into a war, and then as in the Schleswig-Holstein affair, make up his quarrel with Austria; but Bismarck hoped to compel the Italians to make a treaty with him by threatening to maintain the peace if he could not depend upon their support. The fact of the matter was that he proved too cunning for all his opponents. The Austrians played into his hands. They sent a despatch forbidding him any voice in the administration of Holstein to which he made no reply, and his silence they interpreted as a threat, and proceeded to mobilise. This was exactly what Bismarck had looked for. King William was deeply chagrined, and tears filled his eyes when he spoke of the shameful conduct of the Austrian Emperor.

The question at issue between Prussia and Austria now expanded from the mere disposal of the Duchies to the reconstitution of the federal system of Germany. Bismarck declared that the time had come when Germany must receive a new and more effective organisation, and enquired how far Prussia could count on the support of allies if it should be attacked by Austria or forced into war. It was now essential that he should procure an active alliance with the Italians who still demurred. After some delay they finally agreed to sign a treaty to the effect that if Prussia engaged in hostilities with Austria within the next three months they would also declare war. Thus Bismarck had achieved three notable diplomatic victories. He had prevailed upon the King of Prussia to break with Austria, he had made an agreement with France, and he had concluded an alliance with the Italians. Nevertheless, his course was not yet clear. When Austria suddenly proposed a disarming on both sides the King of Prussia turned to his Minister for advice. Bismarck in reply left the decision with his royal master, saying that his own part was prayer rather than counsel, but from the subsequent turn of events it can be taken that his prayers carried with them considerable influence. The mobilisation of the Prussian troops continued, and the Italians were arming. Bismarck in fact was now determined on war, with the reform of the German confederation as the ultimate object in view. In April he proposed that a Parliament should be elected by universal suffrage and direct elections. At first sight it seemed as if the champion of monarchical government had veered round to a democratic theory of government, but in reality he was making an appeal to the peasants and artisans to look up to the King as a common father. In the ensuing war he looked for a direct means of consolidating the confederation, and in this new political venture he saw, to use his own words, "the moral conquest of Germany."

When all hopes of a congress to solve these political problems had faded, Bismarck ordered General Manteuffel to lead his troops into Holstein. On the 12th of June the formal breach between Austria and Prussia was proclaimed by the mutual withdrawal of ambassadors. On the 14th of June the rival motions were placed before the Diet of the Confederation; that of Prussia for the reform of the Federal Constitution, that of Austria for federal execution against Prussia. If the Austrian motion passed Bismarck was determined that Prussia should declare the Confederation at an end, and, in the event of her victory in the coming war, those states of Northern Germany which had voted against her would cease to exist as sovereign states. The Diet agreed to support Austria's motion, and Prussia at once withdrew her delegate from Frankfort, but it is difficult to over-estimate the bitterness of the protest and condemnation that rose from every organ of public opinion, except the military circles of Prussia, against what appeared to be the fratricidal crime of Germans fighting against Germans. On the 15th of May an attempt was made by a young man to take Bismarck's life in the streets of Berlin. Luckily for Bismarck the occurrence served him in good stead. King William, believing his minister's salvation to be a sign of supernatural protection and aid, became more than ever convinced that Prussia was in this crisis the instrument for working out the Divine Will.

The subsequent war told entirely in the favour of Prussian arms. The victory of Sadowa on the 3rd of July won "not only the battle but the campaign," and from that moment the interest centres in diplomatic rather than in military transactions. With Bismarck, who had himself been present at the seat of war, rested the duty of bringing the whole affair to a satisfactory conclusion.

In reality he regarded this encounter with Austria as a mere affair of outposts before the inevitable struggle with France, and having now gained his point he desired to get on friendly terms with Austria in order to be in a position to bring about a war with France, which contingency he believed would alone unite the whole of Germany.

Austria, being in no condition to continue the war, was willing to negotiate terms of peace, but Bismarck for the present did not wish it to appear that Prussia was only aiming at a confederation from which the Southern German States would be excluded. He knew well that Louis Napoleon would give a willing consent to conditions of peace which contained a provision that Germany should be divided into two confederations with the Maine as a boundary. Louis Napoleon's demands at the conclusion of peace amounted, according to Bismarck, to *une politique de pourboire*, that is to say, he desired any territorial acquisition, however unimportant, rather than incur the ridicule of going empty away.

By the Treaty of Prague, which was signed on the 23rd of August 1866, it was arranged that Austria should withdraw from the affairs of Germany. To Prussia was allotted the Duchies,

Hanover, the Electorate of Hesse, a portion of Hesse Darmstadt and the free city of Frankfort. This Treaty forms one of the turning-points in Bismarck's career, for from this moment he changes his *rôle* of party leader, and assumes that of a constructive statesman, and it was in this capacity that he won the hearts of the people. When he returned from the battle-field of Sadowa he found his earlier unpopularity forgotten in the flood of national enthusiasm which his achievements and those of the army had evoked. Even the Parliament of Berlin, in consideration of his avowal that the Cabinet had acted unconstitutionally in raising taxes on their own initiative, consented to forgive the past.

Bismarck now felt that the first step in his great scheme had been taken. He had made Prussia the predominant power, and he had united the North German States. Prussia was strong, therefore he could afford to be generous, and it was by generosity that he hoped to win over the Southern States. His measure for universal suffrage had told in his favour, and the new state wore an air of strength and firmness, now that every German possessed the full right of citizenship, while complete authority rested safely with the council to avoid the obvious dangers of a democracy.

Bismarck, however, was determined, now that his work had begun, to see it through himself. Professing to believe that ministerial responsibility is only possible when there is a single man at the helm who should be brought to task for all mistakes, he arranged that the Chancellor should be the representative of Prussia, and chairman of the council, with powers practically limitless. Holding this supreme office there was only one department over which Bismarck exercised no authority, and that was the army. Nevertheless he had made the State, placed himself at the head of it, given it a Constitution which exists in an almost identical form to the present day, and he had become the most popular figure in Germany, secure against his opponents at home. Henceforward he exerted every effort for the prosperity of Germany, but he knew that it was only in a united Germany that his reforms could work smoothly. There seemed only one chance of union, and that was a war with France, if possible, a war provoked by France; but at present Bismarck was not prepared to adopt a hostile policy.

He even paid an apparently friendly visit to Louis Napoleon in Paris at this very time; but neither side could be blind to the danger ahead.

War was inevitable. Louis Napoleon saw the danger and began seeking for allies. Bismarck saw the danger, and only wished to postpone the crisis until his army was efficient. It was with this very object that he had refused to run any risks over the question of Luxembourg, for there was much to be gained by a little delay. He busied himself instead with a matter which was most essential in his relations with the States of Southern Germany, the completion of the Treaties of Alliance by conventions assimilating the military systems of these states to that of Prussia. A Customs Parliament was established for the whole of Germany, but Bismarck perceiving that the progress towards union was neither so rapid nor so smooth as he had once hoped, did not unduly press on the work of consolidation.

The Spanish question now brought the two countries to the brink of the precipice once again. Bismarck supported the Hohenzollern claims, deeming it to be politically invaluable to have friends in the rear of France, but the King of Prussia at first demurred to give his consent. Finally he gave way, and, had it not been for the fact that a cipher telegram was misinterpreted, Spain would have passed into the hands of a dynasty friendly to Germany. The French people in the meantime had been roused to a pitch of fury in their resentment at Bismarck's machinations, but their remonstrance failed to reach him as he had discreetly retired to "recruit his health in Pomerania." But he wrote to the Prussian agents in Germany protesting that the matter had nothing to do with Prussia, that the Prussian Government had always considered and treated it as one in which Spain and the selected candidate were alone concerned. This may have been literally true, but virtually it was a lie. Bismarck was always ready to seize upon any excuse for war so long as the provocation came from France, and he now believed that his opportunity had at last arrived.

Though we must inevitably condemn the methods he usually employed we cannot help admitting that Bismarck's foreign policy possessed in a supreme degree "the saving virtue of success." He kept silence while the French became more and more incensed with him.

Suddenly came the news that the Hohenzollern Prince had withdrawn his candidature. This would have been a great blow for Bismarck had not the French seemed determined to play into his hands.

Grammont, full of bluster and boast in the hour of his supposed triumph over Germany, was foolish enough to telegraph imperative orders to Benedetti, the French Ambassador at Berlin, to request from the King of Prussia a promise that he would never allow the prince to return to the candidature. Bismarck declared that the Duc de Grammont must either recall or explain the language he had used, and at the same time he intimated to the Crown Prince that under the circumstances war was inevitable. Meanwhile the famous interview between Benedetti and the King was taking place on the esplanade at Ems, in the course of which the King refused the French demands; subsequently telegraphing an account of the proceedings to his Chancellor.

It happened that when Bismarck received the telegram he was dining with Von Roon and Moltke, who both had been summoned to Berlin. The three men were feeling gloomy and depressed at the recent humiliation that, as it seemed to them, their country had suffered. On receiving the message it dawned upon Bismarck that, by publishing its contents, he might have the opportunity he desired for revenge. He at once left the room and drafted a statement keeping to the words of the original text, but omitting much, and so arranging the sentences that they should convey to the readers an impression, not of what had actually occurred, but what he would have wished might have happened. The two other men consented to the scheme, Von Roon assuring Bismarck that the army was in readiness, and Moltke expressing his confidence in the ultimate result. The draft was published late that very night in a special edition of the *North German Gazette*, and at the same time a copy was sent from the Foreign Office to all German Embassies and Legations, with the anticipated result that a storm of indignation arose on all sides and the differences of North and South were swept away. Bismarck's long cherished expectations had been realised, and it mattered not to him by what means, so long as the end was the unity of Germany. He met the King at Brandenburg on his way to Berlin, and after infinite trouble throughout the journey, at the Berlin terminus, he finally induced the King to give the order for mobilisation. The King thereupon gave the order to the Crown Prince, who proclaimed the news to all within earshot. Almost at the same time the order for mobilisation was given in France. There is a noteworthy circumstance in connection with these negotiations which illustrates well the hastiness of the French and the crafty diplomacy of Bismarck. In the Parliament that was now summoned Bismarck was able to announce that the declaration of war from France was the first official communication which throughout the whole affair he had received from the French Government; a circumstance unprecedented in history.

On the 31st of July in the year 1870 Bismarck left Berlin with the King for the seat of war. He was always proud of his *rôle* of soldier, and it came as a welcome relief from office work, benefiting both his health and spirits. From Gravelotte to Sedan he accompanied the victorious army, and he was by the King's side when the French hoisted the white flag upon the citadel. When hostilities had been brought to a conclusion Bismarck violently opposed every scheme of modifying the terms of surrender. The French, he argued, had never forgiven them Sadowa, and it was not likely now that they would ever forgive Sedan. The only circumstances under which the terms might be mitigated would be if the sword which the Emperor surrendered was that of France, but, since the Emperor had declared that it was his own, Moltke was ordered to insist upon the Prussian demands. The scene of these negotiations, which has been so well portrayed in Von Werner's celebrated picture, was one of intense dramatic interest. It was not the first dramatic incident in Bismarck's life, and it was not to be the last, but there have been few conferences of such a nature on which hung so many lives, on

III.] CAPITULATION OF LOUIS NAPOLEON

which such grave issues of international importance depended. The meeting broke up at past midnight. Before daybreak a message arrived from Louis Napoleon craving an interview with Bismarck. The latter complied with the request, and, hastening to the Emperor's carriage at the time appointed, courteously saluted and entered into conversation with him. Louis Napoleon asked if he might see the King, but Bismarck, fearing the Emperor might soften his master's heart, declared it was impossible. He then accompanied Louis Napoleon to a neighbouring cottage, where in the course of conversation he had the audacity to aver that no one wished for the war, that the Germans had looked upon the Spanish affair as Spanish, not German. Nothing of course came of such an interview, and at the neighbouring chateau of Belleville Louis Napoleon signed the capitulation. Bismarck leaving the conference in the hands of military men, who he thought would be harsher, rode up with Moltke to present the capitulation to the King.

In the meantime revolution had broken out in Paris. All the onus of war was thrown upon the unfortunate Emperor, but it suited Bismarck's purpose to regard the whole of the French people as responsible, and to impress it upon the European Powers, and he now demanded both

Metz and Strasburg to secure South Germany against French aggression. At the same time, he avoided negotiations by refusing to recognise the provisional government, although he consented to an interview with Favre. During the interview Bismarck remained obdurate. "Strasburg," he declared, "is the key of our house, and we must have it." Favre on his side protested that he could not discuss conditions which would prove so dishonourable to France, but he forgot that he was dealing with a man who was more than his match at the game of diplomacy. Bismarck rebutted all accusations of cruelty, and like a shrewd statesman carried the war into the enemy's country by bringing up a counter charge against the French for the same offence. These negotiations between Favre and the German Chancellor lasted for several days, and on the 30th of January the Prussian flag waved over the forts of the French capital. Bismarck did not propose immediately to take full advantage of the situation, although the people were now clamouring for the proclamation of the Empire. He could afford to be generous, and he wished the natural sequence of events to work themselves out gradually.

At the court there was some reluctance to assume the imperial title, and it was deemed best that the initiative in this movement should come from the King of Bavaria. Bismarck accordingly addressed a letter to him, in which he pointed out that the defined authority of a German Emperor over Bavaria would be more tolerable than the indefinite claims of a King of Prussia based on a mere superiority of force, and doubtless brought other pressure to bear. The effect was that the Bavarian monarch called upon all the princes to join him in a request to the King of Prussia. On the 18th of January 1871, in the Palace of Versailles, the King publicly assumed the title of Emperor, and two months later the first Parliament of the Empire was opened at Berlin. This then was the consummation of Bismarck's great life-work. He stood now in the zenith of prosperity and glory, the idol of his native land, the terror of France, the fear of every European nation, beyond the reach of envy and untrammelled by political rivalries. The union of the German Empire was recognised as his work alone; there could be little doubt as to the relative merits of the Chancellor and his sovereign. The world has material enough to justify the generally accepted belief that it was the minister who made Germany, and that it was the conspicuous merit of the sovereign, that in spite of many doubts and misgivings, he did, upon a full reckoning, follow the advice and maintain the authority of his chosen servant. There is, of course, every reason to suspect that Bismarck sometimes hurried his master into actions which were repugnant to his feelings, but the sovereign would have utterly missed the road to German unity, had he not been guided by one ever at his side, who brought to him not merely brilliant ideas, but thoroughly matured plans.

On the 10th of May the definite Treaty of Peace was signed at Frankfort. In nine years then Bismarck had completed the great task which he had set himself, and now that he was complete master he did not intend in the fulness of his power to withdraw into untimely seclusion. The great influence which he had acquired after so much effort both at court and in the country at large had become to him the life blood of his existence. In foreign affairs he was at present sole undisputed master, enjoying the complete confidence of the allied sovereigns and the enthusiastic admiration of his fellow-countrymen. He had managed to frustrate all plans for raising a coalition against victorious Germany among the Powers which had been injured by its successes, or whose interests were threatened by its greatness.

His policy was now ostensibly to maintain

peace, but rumour declared that the recuperation of France was so rapid after the war that the German Chancellor feared a war of revenge provoked by the French Government; and both he and Moltke wished to strike before France had again won allies.

Bismarck maintained vigorously in public that he had no warlike intentions, and that all these reports were untrue. But there is no doubt that at the time, even German writers confess, that the plan of attacking France was meditated, and it was a plan of a nature to recommend itself to the military party in Prussia. Moreover, it is now known that in a private interview Gortschakoff warned Bismarck in so many words that the Czar did not desire to see France weakened any further; and it is not likely that such a warning should have been given without very good reason. We are led to the conclusion, then, that if it had not been for the restraining hand of the Czar the policy of peace, which Bismarck professed in public, would have been discarded.

As matters stood, the reconciliation with Austria, which in 1872 had brought the Czar and the Emperor Francis Joseph as guests to Berlin, had made more remote the chance of hostilities, and Europe gradually found herself at rest. For five years the so-called league of the Three Emperors continued in more or less effective existence, condemning France to isolation, and during this interval Bismarck showed himself as great an advocate of peace as he had formerly been of war. Always hating opposition he strove to create a government party which would help him to be the *sine quâ non* of Germany, and which would not necessitate his dependence upon the support of any one political faction. In 1877, however, he wished to resign on the score of ill-health, but the Emperor wrote on the minute of his resignation the peremptory command "Never," while in the Reichstag a great demonstration of confidence in his leadership was displayed on all sides, and with these testimonials of confidence he returned to active life.

In the year 1878 the Eastern question once again threatened serious disputes between the Powers. The national movement which had united Italy and Germany was now infecting the Balkan Peninsula. The many nations concerned, hateful of Mahomedan misrule, turned to Russia as the natural head of a Pan Slavic movement. The failure of the European Concert and the unredressed wrongs of the Balkan Christians drove Russia to declare war on Turkey, but the success of the Russian arms, and the advance on Constantinople, caused general alarm in Europe, which led eventually to the great Congress of Powers in Berlin under the presidency of Bismarck.

"We do not wish," Bismarck commented when this project had been proposed, "to go the way of Napoleon; we do not desire to be arbitrators or schoolmasters of Europe. We do not wish to force our policy on other states by appealing to the strength of our army. I look upon our task as a more useful, though a humbler one; it is enough if we can be an honest broker." The great work that Bismarck achieved at this famous congress was in reconciling the apparently incompatible interests of England and Russia. He it was who acted as conciliator when Gortschakoff folded up his maps, or Lord Beaconsfield ordered a special train. He proved to the world once again that the fortunes of Europe depended on himself, and strengthened a position which was almost unparalleled in the history of Europe.

After Bismarck had succeeded in securing the young Empire against attack from without he turned his attention to social and economic reform within. His domestic policy was marked by a reformed coinage, codification of law, nationalisation of the Prussian railways, repeated increase of the army, and above all a complete revolution in fiscal policy. A serious commercial crisis had occurred in 1873 after one of those great outbreaks of speculation which have from time to time assailed the very foundations of society. Now Bismarck always entertained the strongest aversion to direct taxation. He ascribed the excessive amount of direct taxation to the direct pressure of taxes, and to the fact that men wanted to go to a country where the produce of their labours would be protected against foreign interference. In adopting the policy of Protection Bismarck was influenced, not by economic theory, but by the observation of clearly defined facts. At a time when his colleagues were still convinced Free Traders he already recognised that the doctrines of Free Trade, which seemed enticing enough to the political dilettante and other non-productive consumers, were utterly wrong in practice, and inapplicable to the world of hard facts and business. It was his opinion, after mature consideration, that the policy of free imports had proved a thorough disappointment. Germany was a poor country, and if it was to maintain itself in the modern rivalry of nations it must become rich. It could only become rich through manufactures, and manufacturing industries could not grow without some protection from foreign competition.

The Liberal party, however, remained stubbornly faithful to the old Free Trade doctrine, restricting itself to a barren opposition to all fiscal reform. "Free Trade," Bismarck declared in 1881, "chiefly represents the interests of the seaports, of traders, and a limited number of individuals. Fiscal policy should not be principally shaped so as to suit the interests of certain classes of the population, but should foster the interests of the whole country. It can therefore be criticised with justice only if its effect upon the whole nation is considered." Whatever may be the merits of this argument, after Bismarck had succeeded in re-introducing Protection into Germany the national industries which had been rapidly decaying recovered with amazing rapidity, and within six months factories had doubled the number of their employees, the output of mines and industries largely increased, wages rose with the improving outlook for labour, especially in the iron and coal trades, and the growing deposits in the Savings Banks testified to the success of Bismarck's measure with the masses. True it certainly is that some of the comparatively unimportant branches of industry suffered, and the old cry was raised in some quarters that the new fiscal policy had the effect of increasing the price of the working man's bread. The grain merchants especially could raise a plausible objection when they saw the grain imports from Russia, and therefore their business profits curtailed by the new duties which had been placed upon foreign corn. Bismarck contended that as long as the great corn-growing countries in the East of Europe and over-sea could not sell their surplus production outside Germany, they must pay the corn duties which the German Government imposed, while German merchants had the choice of buying from the various corn-producing countries and from the corn producers at home. Only then would the corn duties have to be paid by the home consumer if the whole production of corn at home and surplus production abroad should be insufficient, or should barely be sufficient to satisfy German requirements. As long as such a scarcity of corn did not arise foreign countries would not, he argued, be able to increase the natural price of corn in Germany, as fixed by the law of supply and demand by the amount of the German corn duty. The chief use of his fiscal policy consisted not in looking after the interest of individual classes but after the economic interests and welfare of the whole German Empire.

It was perhaps inevitable that the opposition should insist that a duty on corn would increase the price of the poor man's bread, but Bismarck contested that much more corn can be grown than is wanted, and therefore the supply is greater

III.]   A NEW POLICY FOR NEW NEEDS   195

than the demand, that the consumers do not run after corn, more being grown than is required, but that the corn producers run after the buyers. Throughout the controversy he insisted that the price of corn and bread did not stand in any relation except in cases of famine. He succeeded in convincing the practical business men of Germany, more especially those engaged in industrial and agricultural pursuits, but he failed to make the German University professors understand that, being unproductive consumers themselves, they had forgotten that the masses of the nation have to "produce" something for them to "consume." Bismarck was shrewd enough to see that the question was not one of exact science as these same German professors, cramped with their fireside reading, had imagined it to be, but rather a question which involved framing a new policy for new needs; a policy which should not be guided by purely technical definitions, but by the test of practical experience.

In these political questions science sometimes rides such a very high horse that it fails to see the ground over which it is riding. Bismarck believed the whole theory of Free Trade to be wrong. He declared that England could step out of the barriers of Protection as it had done, "like a gigantic athlete to challenge the world," because she had become so powerful under the Protectionist *régime*. Free Trade is the weapon of the strongest nation, and England had in the past protected herself against foreign competition with exorbitant protective tariffs until her industries had become so powerful. It is of more than passing interest to Englishmen to observe Bismarck's never-to-be-forgotten utterance in 1879: "England herself is slowly returning to Protection, and by and by she will take it up in order to save for herself at least the home market."

For the rest Bismarck's aims were centred in the establishment of a strong and determined Government, zealously working for the benefit of all classes, looking at each matter as to its effect on the nation as a whole without following a party policy which he condemned as "impossible for a Prussian or a German Minister." At first he encountered much hindrance from his Parliamentary opponents, who he affected to believe did not deserve sufficient respect to be able to injure any one, but national admiration for his past achievements increased year by year, and both by this means and by personal intercourse he was able to put his relations with Parliament on a better footing.

In 1886 he was called upon once again to

bring his powers of diplomacy to the test, when General Boulanger appeared upon the scenes in France to threaten European peace. Bismarck intimated that Germany had no desire for war; "But if France," he added, "has any reason to believe that she is more powerful than we, then war is certain." This was no idle threat. Russia was clamouring for the dismissal of Bismarck or for war, but the German Chancellor deftly played one country off against another. He actually entered into an alliance with Russia, the object of this surprising departure being to prevent Russia from asking help against the Triple Alliance, which itself already secured Germany against attack from Russia. Well might he now declare, "God has put us in a situation in which our neighbours will not allow us to fall into indolence or apathy." But he had saved the German Empire from the grave dangers that threatened her at this crisis.

"It is not fear," he declared in the course of a speech upon the situation, "which makes us lovers of peace, but the consciousness of our own strength. We can be won by love and good-will, but by them alone. We Germans fear God, and nothing else in the world, but it is the fear of God which makes us seek peace and ensue it." This would have been a fitting sentence with which to end a great career, but unfortunately there is another chapter to be told, a chapter remarkable for its very meanness. We must indeed regret for the sake of his own reputation that Bismarck survived so long his great coadjutors in the creation of the German Empire. Some statesmen have gone down to the grave in the fulness of power and popularity. Some have subsided into an honourable retirement to spend the calm evening of a protracted old age in rest and repose after the storm and tempest of an arduous life spent in the service of the State. Some have been cut short in the prime of life at the very beginning of great careers, amid universal tokens of genuine distress. But with Bismarck, alas! it was far otherwise.

In the beginning of the year 1888 the old Emperor died, and in his death Bismarck saw the support on which his power had rested thrust away for ever. A few months later his son, the Emperor Frederick, followed him to the grave. An unfortunate incident, partly domestic partly political, had served to widen the breach indefinitely which had always existed to some extent between Bismarck and this noble member of the House of Hohenzollern. It was the project of marrying Princess Victoria of Prussia and Prince Alexander of Battenberg. Bismarck believed, or affected to believe, that it was a plan concocted by the Empress Frederick to bring over the German Empire to the side of England, so that England might have a stronger support in her standing conflict with Russia.

Bismarck was completely successful in his opposition to the proposal, with the result that there seemed an end of all friendly relations between himself and the Court. The young Emperor William proved himself to be possessed of a strong will and character. Although he always regarded Bismarck with gratitude and admiration, these feelings for the old Chancellor did not hinder him from seriously disagreeing on many important matters of internal policy, and like a young heir who comes into his father's property and is determined to change the former *régime*, he would brook no opposition to his own notions of government.

An inevitable crisis was reached when Bismarck, realising that the Emperor was discussing questions of administration with his colleagues without consulting him, drew the Emperor's attention to the principle of the German Constitution that the Chancellor was responsible for all acts of the Ministers and Secretaries of State. Bismarck felt perhaps that he could safely dare his youthful and inexperienced master to disentangle the threads of European diplomacy without his assistance. If this was his belief he was to be rudely undeceived. The young sovereign answered by a peremptory command that Bismarck should reverse this decree by drawing up a new order. "Then am I to understand, Your Majesty," said Bismarck, speaking in English, "that I am in your way?" A laconic affirmative was all that he could elicit from the Emperor, and the climax was reached on the next day when Bismarck impudently declared that the commands of his sovereign ceased in his wife's drawing-room. This was more than the high-spirited boy-Emperor could tolerate, and the inevitable conclusion to the sordid quarrel was soon reached.

It was a bold stroke of the sovereign's to dismiss the Minister, who was followed by cheering crowds through the streets of Berlin wherever he went, but those who were acquainted with his character knew that one or other must now go, and it was sufficiently patent to all that the one to go must be the subject, not the sovereign. Powerfully as he had affected the imaginations of his contemporaries he certainly overrated his own capacity if he hoped to direct the footsteps of this aspiring youth, and he still more grossly mistook his own disposition if he thought that he could long act in concert with the new generation.

But his was a great fall. It is not every day that the savage hatred of envious men is gratified by the agonies of such a spirit and the overshadowing of such a name; but so fell the Iron Chancellor. He left Berlin to spend the remainder of his life in ignominious and inevitable retirement, displaying a malicious temperament to which the behaviour of Napoleon at St Helena is the only parallel in history. For the rest of his life he busied himself with developing the very worst side of his character. Nothing that his successors did was right. He embarrassed the Government with paltry criticisms, and he impaired the influence of the nation by injuring the reputation of the Ministry; he refused to be present at Moltke's funeral; and although the Emperor did his best to make up his quarrel with him, Bismarck never ceased to contrast the young Emperor with the old, very much to the detriment of the former. His sayings and his writings reveal a child-like petulance which the meanest of mankind would be ashamed to display. "After all," he querulously whimpers, "who are these Hohenzollerns? My family is as good as theirs. We have been here longer than they have."

And yet with all these faults we cannot withhold from him our sympathy during his great trial; and however much his behaviour is to be deplored, the heavy clouds that overhung the sunset of his life cannot obliterate the memory of that brilliant noontide. He found himself quite unable to settle down to any quiet pursuit. To him the whirlwind of the political hurricanes were as the very atmosphere of existence, and under the burden of his grievances he slowly fretted away the few remaining months of his life. On the 31st July, in the year 1898, he passed away at Friedrichsruhe, where he was laid to rest by the few intimate friends and relatives who kept with him to the end.

It is always a difficult task to dissociate the personal character of a great statesman from his public actions. The interest excited by the events of his career mingles itself in our minds with that which properly belongs to a scrutiny of his moral qualities. It is very obvious that Bismarck possessed all the essentials of a great man, some in a less, some in a greater degree. No one can deny that certain glaring faults must temper the admiration of the most enthusiastic, but equally no one can deny that his questionable actions possessed all those features which distinguish the errors of magnanimous and intrepid spirits from those of base and malignant men. Although it has been maintained that flexibility of principle however serviceable can never be respectable, yet all allowance must be made for the wear and tear which honesty necessarily sustains in the friction of political life. The trait in his character which attached most opprobrium to his name was his intolerance of all those who set stumbling-blocks in his path, or who in any way opposed him. He dealt out merciless castigations right and left to those who disagreed with his own views on any subject whatever. "When I have my enemy in my hands I must destroy him," he once said to Count Beust, and this sentence admirably sums up the character of his policy. But his greatness chiefly consisted in the determination to obtain his ends in spite of all opposition. "Take care of that man," said Disraeli on one occasion, referring to Bismarck, " he means what he says."

His aim was the union and welfare of his native land, and if he committed grave breaches of conventional moral codes, and resorted to the harshest measures for this purpose, it was because he was discerning enough to see that the maladies of State were beyond the reach of gentle remedies, and his sins are to some extent condoned by that motive which alone can in some measure excuse deviation from the paths of strict morality, the good of his countrymen. He redeemed great faults by the firmness, energy and dauntless courage which characterised his every action, although it is to be regretted that he acted on many occasions with inexcusable severity towards his opponents, even descending to take advantage of the law of libel to confound them. His jealousy of those with whom he worked made all real co-operation impossible. He would explain and justify his policy to the King alone. Von Roon said of him that he always wished to do everything himself, and issued the strictest orders that he was never to be disturbed. Any criticism on the Constitution or upon German policy he regarded as a personal insult. He would allow no superior but the King, in fact the devotion which he professed to his sovereign may be accounted for in part by the fact that he knew there could be no competition between himself and his master. With all his love of power, with the jealousy and vindictiveness that have left some very grievous blots on his reputation, his ambitions were indeed legitimate, and his aims undeniably patriotic. His love of his country was a jealous love, and he was jealous of others who might, if it were possible, love her better than he did.

Perhaps the most remarkable feature in the man was the religious side of his character. For him Christianity and monarchy were inseparably bound up together. "If I were not a Christian I would be a Republican," he once remarked, meaning that he could only obey a king if a king held his authority as the representative of a higher power. The king, he argued, owed his power to the people or to God; there could be no compromise. He refused to believe that the voice of the people was the voice of God: "For me the words 'by the grace of God,' which Christian rulers add to their names are no empty phrase; I see in them a confession that princes desire to wield the sceptre which God has given them according to the will of God on earth. As the will of God I can only recognise that which has been revealed in the Christian Gospel. I believe that the realisation of Christian teaching is the end of the State." How deep-rooted his religious convictions were, it is possible to determine from several sources. His profession of faith has been aptly termed a "muscular Christianity," but in truth it did not lack the more tender touches of an earnest soul. Witness his own words: "I would to God," he once exclaimed, "that besides what is known to the world I had not other sins upon my soul, for which I can only hope for forgiveness, in a confidence in the blood of Christ," and again, "If among the multitude of sinners who are in need of the glory of God, I hope that His grace will not deprive me of the staff of humble faith which I endeavour to find out of my path. If I were not a strict believing Christian, if I had not the miraculous basis of religion, you would never have lived to see such a Bund-Chancellor." Surely these are words born of true and deep conviction. It is related that before his duel with Vinche he received the sacrament, and that his adversary refused to fire upon him, as he had noticed that Bismarck was engaged in prayer. Motley's account of him also seems to endorse the opinion that he was sincere—"strict integrity and courage of character, a high sense of honour, a firm religious belief." Bismarck himself inserted the following sentence into one of his own letters: "If I were to live without God I do not know why I should not put life aside like a dirty shirt!" Undoubtedly there was in him the fear of God; this was the first great principle of his life; the second was his reverence for the monarchy, and the combination of the two produced in him an ardent patriotism, a patriotism which saw in the unity and welfare of his country, the noblest effect of the teaching of his God.

With regard to his powers of oratory, it must be admitted that he was deficient in physical gifts, and yet he possessed to some degree the solemnity and gesture of a great speaker. His orations were carefully prepared. He was an admirable debater. He displayed in his speaking a vivid imagination, an unequalled power of illustration, the thought was always concrete, and he was never satisfied with the vague ideas and abstract conceptions which so clearly moved his contemporaries. Complete absence of affectation characterised his public utterances, and he was wont to express his ideas in words so forcible and original that they were thoroughly impressed on his audience.

Much the same may be said of his writing; there have been few better writers in history. In official despatches he was opposed to the system of saying much and meaning little. His argument in these epistles were always clear, complete and concise; and for closeness of reasoning, wealth of knowledge, and cogency of argument they will remain as monuments in the history of literature. His power of work was marvellous, but his constitution suffered thereby. He was of a highly nervous and irritable temperament, and it is said of him that in early youth there was in his nature a morbid restlessness, a dissatisfaction with himself which he tried to still, but only increased by wild excesses. This feature in his character exhibits itself in a marked way throughout his career, and combined with nervous irritation greatly interfered with his official labours. On one occasion at St Petersburg it occasioned a malady which is said to have expelled the good humour which he displayed in earlier years. To such lengths was he driven by this ungovernable passion that on the occasion of his interview with the King of Prussia to discuss the congress at Frankfort to settle the Schleswig-Holstein question, he smashed a trayful of glasses on the table to relieve his feelings. The result of this nervous temperament was that he possessed little self-control, and he developed in consequence that truculency of manner which is responsible for many a hostile interpretation of his character. No man can attain unpopularity with greater ease than one who, to use the conventional colloquism, "lays down the law." Bismarck had a peculiarly irritating way of doing so. From early youth onwards he was ever deficient in ready obedience to authority, which in men of smaller minds and less influence is a grave hindrance to success. It was perhaps excusable in his case, but his popularity was not thereby enhanced.

In his diplomatic negotiations Bismarck, like Cavour, acted upon the theory that even when there is good cause to keep things doubtful or dark there is no blind like the truth. With this affectation of frankness that was blunt almost to brutality no one could suspect him of diplomacy. His frankness appeared to the French people "a sort of ironical challenge addressed to their credulity." With a remarkable self-belief, pride of caste, and withal insolently aggressive, the *rôle* of courtier and counsellor to his sovereign seemed strangely paradoxical to the outside world; but it was not by the subtleties and delicacies of the conventional diplomatist that he won his way, it was by sheer brute strength. While some statesmen have been comparable to graceful edifices he was the firm rough rock; jagged and uncomely perhaps, but strong to resist the full force of adverse wind and tide. It was another notable characteristic of his diplomacy that he would generally keep in his mind several different plans so that if one failed he would adopt another; in this acting upon Napoleon's maxim, "Always have two strings to your bow." But he was withal cautious.

In foreign policy although he seemed bold and decisive he did not lack those qualities of caution and prudence which are the essential attributes of a statesman. To these he owed his success. He could strike when the time came, but he rarely did so until he had taken stock of his surroundings. He never began a war unless he was confident of the ultimate issue and, unlike Louis Napoleon, he left nothing to chance or good fortune. In internal affairs perhaps he was less prudent: he exaggerated his own influence, and he can hardly be freed from the charge of opportunism. He tried to govern Germany in a series of political alliances, and it is to be feared that he thought rather more of the alliance than the permanent effect it might produce; but all his public work is marked by the same intellectual resource, originality and common sense.

He had such a superb fashion of treating questions. His ideas and his plans were always large, and at the same time his speculations had none of that vagueness so characteristic of political philosophers. What he did he did thoroughly, even if it were necessary to use violence. None ever destroyed more ruthlessly than Bismarck, but he belonged to a school that banished sentiment from politics, and it must always be remembered that whenever he destroyed it was with a view to replace what was effete with solid and durable materials, and to prepare the way for his own magnificent schemes of reconstruction.

While his country was in danger he adopted a resolute and uncompromising attitude, holding that when an extreme case called for that remedy which is in its own nature most violent, and which is only a remedy because it is violent, it would be idle to think of mitigating or diluting. We can readily detect in such maxims the teaching of Machiavelli. There is a certain passage in the "Prince" which runs something after this fashion:

"The manner in which we live and that in which we ought to live, are things so wide asunder that he who quits the one to betake himself to the other is more likely to destroy than save himself, since anyone who would act up to a certain standard of goodness in everything must be ruined among so many who are not good."

Thousands of human beings who have never heard of the name of Machiavelli have excused their immoral actions on this same score, although it does not constitute an excuse but rather an explanation. It is not sufficient to excuse the bad in Bismarck, because those with whom, and against whom he worked were bad men. It hardly constitutes an explanation. We will not attempt here to deny Bismarck's enormities, but let us bear in mind that the course which, on close inspection seems so tortuous, may from a loftier point of view appear straight and direct. Let us remember that his own ambitions paled before his love of country and his loyalty to the King. He found glory only because glory lay in the path of duty, that he placed before all personal considerations, the duty which he, as the jealous and implacable guardian of German greatness felt bound to perform. It was the ambition of Bismarck to raise the German name throughout the world to a pre-eminence it had not enjoyed since the Hohenstaufens, and it was because his ambition coincided with the national instinct of the German race that this great result was achieved.

It has often been contested that Bismarck's conception of a German Empire was merely a military despotism, limiting the duty of Parliament to the voting of supplies, that the welding together of the various states resulted in a defensive league from which Prussia alone could reap any benefit, that this unification was brought about at the expense of individual liberty, and that the country has been created for the Emperor, not the Emperor for the country; but it must be remembered that although German union under the House of Hohenzollern was established by the policy of "blood and iron," such means were fit for reformation's sake.

It was the work of Bismarck to direct the sentimental patriotism of the German people to practical ends, and to convert their vague aspirations into solid and enduring realities. Confident in the Divine Providence which he unquestionably believed to be specially favourable to himself, he achieved this task, and inspired his countrymen with high ambitions. As long as the German Empire lasts, the memory of his majestic figure and intrepid spirit will never fade.

INDEX

A

AMERICA, 52
Augustenberg, Duke of, in Schleswig-Holstein dispute, 166, 167, 168; interview with Bismarck, 169, 170; Bismarck announces his claim, 171; d'Azeglio, Massimo, 89, 91, 92, 98, 107

B

BALBO, COUNT CESARE, 85
Balkan Peninsula, 190
Battenberg, Prince Alexander of, 198
Baudin, 58
Bavaria, 187
Bazaine, Marshal, 62
Beauharnais, Hortense, 8, 10
Belleville, Castle of, 185
Benedetti, Count, 182
Beranger, 14
Berlin, 150, 151, 154, 187
Biarritz, 50, 173
Bismarck, early years, 146, 147, 148, 149; enters New Assembly, 150, 151; at Diet of Frankfort, 152, 153, 154; in Paris, 155; at St Petersburg, 156, 157, 158; as Foreign Minister, 159, 160, 162, 163, 164; and the Schleswig-Holstein dispute, 165, 166, 167, 168, 169, 170, 171, 172; interview with Louis Napoleon, 173; breach with Austria, 174, 175; victory of Sadowa, 176; the Treaty of Prague, 177, 178; supreme in office, 179; the Spanish question, 180, 181; the Ems telegram, 182; declaration of war with France, 183;

the Franco-Prussian War, 184, 185, 186; union of the German Empire, 187; peace with France, 188; league of the Three Emperors, 189; the Eastern question and the Congress of Berlin, 190, 191; fiscal policy, 192, 193, 194, 195, 196; alliance with Russia, 197; quarrel with the Court, 198, 199, 200; his fall, 201; his death, 202; his character, 203, 204, 205, 206, 207, 208, 209, 210, 211, 212
Blessington, Lady, 11
Bologna, 99, 100
Boulanger, General, 97
Boulogne, 12
Bülow, Count von, 149
Buol, Count, 109, 110
Buonaparte, Jerome, 106
—— Louis, 8
—— Napoleon, 8

C

CALABRIA, 121
Canrobert, Marshal, 32
Cavaignac, 18
Cavour, early years, 78, 79, 80, 81, 82; visit to England, 83, 84; edits *Il Risorgimento*, 85, 86, 87; proclamation of Moncalieri, 88; Minister of Commerce, 89; plans to eject Austria from Italy, 90, 91; forms ministry, 92; reforms in Piedmont, 93, 94, 95; the Crimean War, 96; trouble with the Vatican, 97; the Congress of Paris, 98, 99, 100, 101; takes over Foreign Office, 102; alliance with Louis

INDEX

Cavour (*continued*)—
Napoleon, 103, 104, 105, 106, 107, 108, 109; war with Austria, 110, 111, 112; Villafranca, 113; resigns office, 114, 115; cession of Nice and Savoy, 116, 117; Garibaldi's expedition, 118, 119, 120, 121, 122, 123; Italy united, 124; question of Rome as Capital, 125, 126; death, 127, 128; character, 129, 130, 131, 132, 133, 134, 135, 136, 137, 138, 139, 140, 141, 142
Chambord, Comte de, 23
Changarnier, General, 21
Charlotte, Empress, 53
Chislehurst, 63
Christian of Glücksberg, 166, 170
Clarendon, Lord, 100, 101
Clotilde, Princess, 106, 141
Conneau, Dr, 99, 105
Coup d'état of Louis Napoleon, 25, 26, 27, 28, 29
Cowley, Lord, 47
Crimean War, 31, 32, 33, 96

D

Derby, Lord, 108
Disraeli, Mr, 158, 191, 203
Drouyn, de Lluys, Mons., 35

E

Ems, 58, 182
Eugenie, Empress, 33, 59, 62, 63

F

Favre, 186
Fleury, 19
Francis, King of Naples, 100, 118, 119, 120, 121
—— Joseph, of Austria, and the armistice of Villafranca, 43, 113; cedes Venetia, 51; makes peace with France, 156; league of the three Emperors, 189
Frankfort, 152, 154, 188
Frederick, Crown Prince of Germany, 164, 167, 183, 198
—— VII. of Denmark, 166
Friedrichsruhe, 202

G

Garibaldi, first interview with Cavour, 102; Cavour solicits his aid, 107; his dealings with Cavour, 111; expedition to liberate Sicily and Naples, 118, 119, 120; enters Naples, 121, 122; opposes Cavour, 123; yields to Victor Emmanuel's wishes, 124; relations with Cavour, 132, 133
Gastein, 172
Genoa, 118
Ginlay, General, 112
Gortschakoff, 189, 191
Göttingen, 147
Grammont, Duc de, 57, 181, 182
Gravelotte, 62, 184
Greville, 10
Guizot, 14, 116

H

Ham, Fortress of, 12
Hugo, Victor, 27

I

Isabella of Spain, 57

K

Kiel, 169
Kleist, 149
Kreuz Zeitung, 149

L

La Farina, Giuseppe, 102
La Marmora, 114
Lamoricière, 122
Lauenberg, 172
Lauza, 103
Leopold of Hohenzollern, 57
Leri, 80, 82
Lombardy, 113
Louis Napoleon, early years, 7, 8, 9, 10, 11; lands at Boulogne, 12; the 1848 revolution, 13, 14, 15; takes his seat in the Constituent Assembly, 16, 17;

INDEX

Louis Napoleon (*continued*)—
President, 18, 19, 20, 21, 22, 23, 24 ; the *coup d'état*, 25, 26, 27, 28 ; becomes emperor, 29 ; the Crimean War, 30, 31, 32, 33 ; the Empire at its zenith, 33, 34 ; opinion of Drouyn de Lluys, 35, 36, 37 ; the Orsini outrage, 37, 38 ; Italian policy, 39, 40, 41, 42, 43, 44 ; relations with the Pope, 45 ; annexation of Nice and Savoy, 46, 47, 48 ; the Polish insurrection, 49 ; Schleswig - Holstein, 50, 51 ; the Mexican fiasco, 52, 53, 54 ; outwitted by Bismarck, 55, 56, 57, 58 ; Franco-Prussian War, 59, 60, 61 ; death, 63 ; character, 64, 65, 66, 67, 68, 69, 70, 71, 72, 73
Louis Philippe, 14
Luxembourg, 14

M

MACMAHON, 62
Magenta, 42, 112
Magnan, 19
Malmesbury, Lord, 91
Manteuffel, General, 175
Marie Louise, 8
Mars-la-Tour, 62
Marsala, 119
Maupas, 19, 25
Maximilian, Emperor, 52, 53, 54
Messina, 120
Metz, 61, 62, 186
Milazzo, 120
Mirafiori, Countess, 103
Moltke, 182, 183, 184, 189
Mont Cenis Tunnel, 103
Morny, 19, 25

N

NAPLES, 118, 120, 121, 124
National Assembly of France, Louis Napoleon's message to, 16 ; his oath in, 18 ; change of ministers in, 22 ; and the *coup d'état*, 23, 24 ; dissolved by proclamation, 26
Ney, Colonel, 17
Nicholas, Emperor of Russia,

declines to acknowledge Louis Napoleon, 30 ; and the King of Prussia, 154 ; Bismarck's friendly relations, 162, 163 ; brings forward Duke of Oldenburg in Schleswig - Holstein dispute, 169 ; league of the three Emperors, 189
Novara, 87

O

OLDENBERG, DUKE OF, 169
Orsini, Felice, 37, 38, 103, 105

P

PALERMO, 119
Palestro, 112
Palmerston, Lord, and Louis Napoleon, 43 ; enraged with Louis Napoleon's Italian policy, 47, 48 ; his friendship with Cavour, 92 ; his friendship cools, 101, 102 ; admires Cavour's enterprise, 103
Paris, Congress of, 98, 99
Pelissier, General, 32
Persano, Admiral, 120
Persigny, 16, 19
Piedmont, Cavour's object-lesson, 84 ; Cavour's reforms, 92, 93 ; and the Congress, 108, 109, 110 ; demand for union with Piedmont, 112
Plombières, 39, 46, 105
Poland, 49, 50, 161, 162
Potsdam, 159
Prague, Treaty of, 177

R

RAGLAN, LORD, 32
Rattazzi, 91, 115, 116
Ripon, Lord, 84
Rocca, General della, 104
Rochefort, Mons., 61
Romagna, 8
Rome, 92, 123, 124, 125, 126
Roon, Von, 157, 159, 182, 183
Russell, Lord Odo, 107

S

Saarbrucken, 62
Sadowa, 176
Sardinia, 95, 104, 119
Savoy, 44, 106, 116, 117
Schleswig - Holstein, and Louis Napoleon, 50; history of the dispute, 165, 166; Bismarck's part in the dispute, 167, 168, 169, 170; Austrian policy, 171, 172, 173; the duties allotted to Prussia, 177
Schönhausen, 146, 148
Sedan, 62, 184
Sicily, 118, 120, 121
Solferino, 42, 113
Spicheren, 62
St Arnaud, Marshal, 19, 23, 25
Strasburg, 10, 61, 186
Switzerland, 10

T

Tchernaia, battle of, 96
Teano, 125
Thiers, Mons., 14, 17, 27, 58
Thouvenel, Mons., 46
Ticino, 112
Tuileries, 15, 29
Turin, 78, 79, 124

V

Vatican, Cavour's policy, 97; the French garrison upholds Pope, 105; question of Pope's domination, 123, 124, 125, 126
Venetia, 113
Versailles, 187
Vienna, Treaty of, 170
Victor Emmanuel, sounds Louis Napoleon, 39, 41; and Cavour's resignation, 91, 92; Crimean War, 94; visits England, 97; fear of Cavour, 98; quarrel with Cavour, 103; and the Orsini episode, 104; alliance with Louis Napoleon, 108; war against Austria, 112; Villafranca, 113, 114; and Naples, 119; and Garibaldi, 123, 124; relations with Cavour, 131
Victoria, Queen, 34, 97
Victoria of Prussia, Princess, 198
Villafranca, 43, 113

W

Walewski, 46, 100
Weissenberg, 62
Wilhelmshohe, 63
William I., Emperor of Germany, refuses to interfere with Spanish question, 57; fears Bismarck's policy, 149, 150, 151; treats with Austria, 154; breaks down, 156; asks Bismarck's advice, 157; sends Bismarck to Paris, 158; appoints Bismarck Foreign Minister, 159; the Schleswig-Holstein dispute, 172, 173, 174; war with Austria, 176; the Franco-Prussian war, 184; proclaimed Emperor, 187; his death, 198
Worth, 62

Z

Zurich, peace of, 115